CW01305707

RECREATING REALITY

Change the way you look at the world
and the world changes.

R. RYAN QUESTEL

Copyright © 2014 R. Ryan Questel.

All rights reserved. No part of this book may be reproduced, stored, or transmitted by any means—whether auditory, graphic, mechanical, or electronic—without written permission of both publisher and author, except in the case of brief excerpts used in critical articles and reviews. Unauthorized reproduction of any part of this work is illegal and is punishable by law.

ISBN: 978-1-4834-2356-2 (sc)
ISBN: 978-1-4834-2355-5 (e)

Because of the dynamic nature of the Internet, any web addresses or links contained in this book may have changed since publication and may no longer be valid. The views expressed in this work are solely those of the author and do not necessarily reflect the views of the publisher, and the publisher hereby disclaims any responsibility for them.

Any people depicted in stock imagery provided by Thinkstock are models, and such images are being used for illustrative purposes only.
Certain stock imagery © Thinkstock.

Lulu Publishing Services rev. date: 12/30/2014

Contents

Foreword vii
Acknowledgements ix
Introduction xi

Chapter 1: Know Thy Self 1
    Who Am I Really? 1
    The Man in the Mirror 6
    The Construct 10
    Energy 15

Chapter 2: What Is Real, Really? 19
    The 5 Senses 19
    The Sixth Sense 22
    Family 26
    The Earth 30

Chapter 3: Things We Say & Do 34
    Everyday Language 34
    Why We Do the Things We Do 38
    Insanity 42

Chapter 4: Law 47
    Maritime Admiralty Law 47
    Courts & Legalese 51

    Conditional Acceptance 55
    Contracting 59

Chapter 5: Money 65
    Is Money Real? 65
    Debt 70
    Banks 74
    Alternative Money 79

Chapter 6: Corporations 83
    Greed Is Good? 83
    Control 87

Chapter 7: The Government 92
    Does Government Work? 92
    Politics 98

Chapter 8: The News 102
    Corporate Media 102
    Fear Factor 106

Chapter 9: Religious Beliefs 111
    Ancient Religion 111
    Gods 118
    Our Hidden Past 123

Chapter 10: Free Your Mind 128
    Community & Trust 128
    Freedom 132
    Reality Check 138

Quotes from Recreating Reality 145

Foreword

In the last six years I have been immersed in an eye opening and self empowering journey of information with a totally unknown destination. This journey has been fuelled only by curiosity and has been continuously and phenomenally inspiring. I hope with your participation you might have a glimpse of this world as I now see it, one which I would have never thought existed if not for my tenacious personality in my search for answers. A world without limits, only plateaus, where the sky is not the final destination as we have been told and you are the architect of your own consciousness and being.

I have had an inquisitive mind for as long as I can remember and, although we have all been taught to follow traditions and culture by our parents and society, I deemed to always question the status quo. My initial quest for answers came from the unsatisfactory opinions received from religion; instead I began to seek out facts over beliefs. This research further lead me onto law, politics, physics, psychology and philosophy. Although I have not pursued a degree in any of the above disciplines my insatiable thirst for knowledge kept me researching and reading everything I could find on the subjects, that I may eventually understand the reason for why things are the way they are, and also where I fit in this equation we call life.

My views expressed in this book on law are based on fact; taken directly from reputable law dictionaries and statutes; acts and bills in active force. I have also put these findings into practice successfully which I highly recommend you verify for yourself by doing your own extensive research by reading various acts of legislation i.e. "The Road Traffic Act 1988" and "The Bills of Exchange Act 1882" as well looking into the meanings of legal definitions. The evidence compiled over the years is accurate information. You will find it impossible to dispute when investigated but this should not be received or taken as legal advice as I do not practice law. You will soon come to realise this is just the tip of the iceberg so I believe you should use the information throughout this book as a source of inspiration and a guide to your own path in seeking the truth. Although you may not agree with every aspect of literature you read here, that's okay. It is not my intention to try to convince you of anything; much of it is just my interpretation of how I see the world we live in. With this in mind, I do hope I can somehow spark your curiosity enough to ultimately open a new spectrum of paradigms and a shift in consciousness towards new ideas and solutions for creating a greater world.

> "Those who are able to see beyond the shadows and lies of their culture will never be understood, let alone believed, by the masses."
>
> **Plato**

> "Reality exists in the human mind, and nowhere else."
>
> **George Orwell - 1984**

Acknowledgements

This book is dedicated to a great man, a teacher that made a lasting impression upon me and was largely responsible for the person I am today.

My Grandfather
Ramondo "Papa" Lares
1919 - 2001

Introduction

Born in the early seventies, not long after the "Black Power Movement", in the Caribbean Island of Trinidad to parents with as diverse an ancestry as the country itself, R. Ryan Questel almost didn't survive shortly after his birth. He had a near death experience in the Port-Of-Spain General Hospital and if it were not for a stranger, an old woman who remarkably diagnosed his symptoms after only briefly speaking to his distressed mother once. A woman who she never saw again.

He emigrated to London at the age of twenty-four and it was here gaining the ability to travel unhindered he began experiencing different people, cultures and beliefs which fuelled and ever growing inquisitiveness in mankind existence and the social order. The choices made throughout his life are proceeding astute views he holds compared to the narrative generally accepted by society, although he will refrain from being categorised or labelled as a rebel, activist or as any other connotations of this or of any kind.

The main concern of his is the imbalance in the world, in social injustice and mankind's apathetic behaviour and disregard toward nature. His goal is for a total restructure in ones consciousness that could possibly lay a pathway toward living in a state of equilibrium with the Earth, in peace and total freedom, justice and equality for all, everywhere.

Chapter 1

Know Thy Self

Who Am I Really?

A question that is asked by the most intellectual and philosophers alike, often by the ignorant and those seeking knowledge of self but it is a question that only you can truly answer yourself. Man or woman, in these times who can really define you or anyone for that matter? Only you can decide who you really are or who you will become. There's not a man, woman or institution that can without a doubt prove nor disprove who you are or who you claim to be unless you agree with them or if there somehow exists irrefutable evidence that suggests otherwise.

When life begins, what we are told is that we are an infant, in this instance let's say an infant boy who's given a name by his parents like Tom, Dick or Harry. We inherit our parents family name or title, we then get the birth registered at a government registry office and a certificate of birth is created for the child because that's what we were told to do and if we don't do so within a specific time, in some countries you can be fined. It is amazing that people never question what exactly the purpose of a birth certificate is. To my surprise most people, if not all, believe it's for:

(1) Proving My Identity. Well that's funny because if you look carefully at the "Certificate" (see legal definition) you will notice written on it at least here in the UK are the words "Not To Be Used As Identification" Huh? But isn't this the same document that's requested when:

(2) Applying For Child Benefits or For a Passport Or Drivers Licence? Well if it's not ID then what is it and why do they need to see it? Now I just went and opened a large can of brain eating worms, didn't I?

Ok, now the problem is that the birth certificate which is said to be proof of birth therefore is supposed to be proof of who I am, right? Wrong! See I am the reason the certificate was created, I brought that document into existence, without me it cannot and would not exist, so how could it now have power over me, the power to confirm and determine to government agents or anyone for that matter who I am. Confused? Ok let me ask a different question. Who has power over whom the Creator or the Created? The answer is obvious now, right? Well it is if you believe in God. So this piece of paper is of no significance as it cannot make any affirmation of any kind as to whoever I am, or claim to be, unless I and only I say that piece of paper is me. After all am I not a living, breathing form of life, capable of intelligent thought and reasoning, with blood flowing through my veins representing a soul? Or am I some ink on a piece of paper? Then how dare they assume that paper can possibly be me?

I know what's happening to you right now, those little brain eating worms are munching away in your head and I think you might need an aspirin, quick. Alright, here is another way to look at it. Let's say you've just bought a brand new car straight out of the factory, a beautiful silver ride, 18" rims with full leather interior. It's not registered yet so there is no certificate. Who owns the car? How can you prove you own it? You bought it, so where's your proof? Give up yet? Your proof of purchase, which is your receipt of course. So now, you've registered the car with the DVLA, and you get your certificate in the mail. Sweet! But wait, it says that you're now the registered "Keeper" huh? So by "Registering" your vehicle, you've just changed your "Title" as the "Certificate" implies. To put it in simple terms to "Register" a thing is to give up "Title" or you can say "Ownership" to then become who is in "Care" of that thing, understand? Basically you did not want the responsibility to manage your own affairs so the government says 'come on down, we'll do it for you but you have got to agree to our terms and conditions. In-turn we will allow you certain benefits and privileges'. Well they don't exactly say that to you but they assume you know that's how it works. Everything in the legal world works on assumptions and if you don't know they'll assume you know what you're getting yourself into. There is an important legal principle that says ignorance of the law is no excuse.

So it's that simple, you're an "Equitable Asset" and the answer to the function of a birth certificate is our third option:

(3) "Debt Capital Instrument". What happens is they issue these "Instruments" which are a type of "Bond" which in turn will be used to raise funds, basically borrow money from the central banks to run the country. So to put it one way is you're owned. Well, yes and no. The thing is you the natural person cannot be owned but your artificial 'Person' can. I can literally see those brain eating worms wriggling around your head again. My person you say! Yep your 'Person'. You see your 'Person' is not you but you believe it is you and it can be you if you want it to be. The problem is that people

don't know they have a 'Person' nor do they know what a 'Person' in the legal world is so they believe they are the person. There is what you call a Natural Person that's what you are of flesh and blood, a body and soul, living and breathing and the Artificial Person i.e. a corporation. I suggest you look up the definition in a law dictionary.

The Natural Person which you are and always will be is always in possession of inalienable rights, granted by the creator, let's say God. And only God can take them away, you heard me right only God, on the other hand The Artificial Person is only entitled to certain benefits and privileges that are given and can be taken away by its creator. So who created this artificial person you ask? Well let's look at how it came about, remember when your parents took you down to that government building to get you registered and a birth certificate was created, abracadabra! Poof! Your artificial person has now been created, with the same name as you and that's why you think the name on the certificate is you but it's not, nope not you. You know how you can tell the difference? The imposter's name will always be written in full capitals on your government document or in other words 'Capitis Diminutio Maxima'.

Well what that means is the creator of the artificial person, allowing you certain benefits and privileges can only be, yep you guessed it, the government, with your parents' unwitting help of course. So what has been created now is what's called a "Trust" where you are the Beneficiary/Shareholder and Director of that account because you're the one bringing the equitable asset, which is your human body. So that leaves the government as the Trustees giving them only limited authority over the trust. But what is done is a flipping of the script on us, they make you believe the opposite by making them beneficiary/shareholder and director and you the trustee. The crafty little devils. So any ID, Document, Letter, P.C.N. Contract, Bill, Invoice etc. with that name appearing on it is not you the Natural Person. A conspiracy! No not really. It's only good business being practiced by our own leaders to generate capital for the economy, but were just not told this, and why would they tell us? It's a sweet deal. Looking up legal definitions which I strongly recommend, will help you along the way understanding what is really being done to you in your everyday interactions with the system and only then you will start to see the system for what it really is and what the artificial person created by the government purpose is really for, and that is to engage you in the world of Commerce.

"To know thyself is the beginning of wisdom."

Socrates

Black's Law Dictionary

Capitis diminutio maxima: The highest or most comprehensive loss of status. This occurred when a man's condition was changed from one of freedom to one of bondage, when he became a slave.

The Man in the Mirror

"I am" is the response God gave to Moses when he asked "what is the name I should give to them". Not that I'm religious but this is a good example of explaining who you really are. You are basically you, no more, no less, whoever you claim to be is also you and if anyone claims otherwise they must literally provide proof in some way, shape or form, to rebut any claim you make. Besides, who knows you better than you, right? Anyone that claims you are the Artificial Person is a corporate entity engaging in commerce looking to "Contract" or wanting an "Agreement" (see legal definition) with them for one purpose, your hard earned money. The easiest way to explain the Artificial Person is to ask you to look in the mirror. See that reflection? Well that's your person. Your reflection is not you, it is a reflection of you so if I hit it you won't feel it, obviously. But if I charge it with a penalty of say £50 and make you believe the reflection is you then you will pay it no problem, but if you knew the laws that commerce are bound by then your circumstances change. When you get over the fact that you are a natural person and not the artificial person the first thing you then need to know is how to enforce that fact. So how exactly do we go about doing that?

(1) Knowing which laws apply to the Natural Person and which apply to the Artificial Person.

Constitutional Law Vs. Statute Law. As a natural person we have the right to engage with other natural persons. To exchange goods for other goods or services is called barter, as practiced in the earlier days. Once cash was introduced, services were no longer needed in exchange for goods or vice versa. Payment was given in gold or silver which still wasn't a bad deal because we could still exchange it and get food if we didn't have a particular skill or product to offer. But in those days everyone grew their own crops and/or owned livestock so money wasn't used or needed by everyone. Later on when corporations started mass producing and engaging in commerce these transactions had to be regulated and controlled for many reasons. Therefore 'Legislature' created 'Legislations', 'Statutes' and 'Acts' of parliament (see legal definition). These had to be written in as laws giving them authority over its practice but statutory laws remained subordinate and always will be to the higher constitutional laws of the land.

(2) Court Procedure

If you are invited to go to court to defend yourself, don't. It's a trap to get you to agree to being the artificial person. But if you think you know your stuff or just want to experience what a joke the court system is, first make sure you're in the right court. What do I mean? The Crown Court is a statute court practicing statute law so if you're planning on going in there with constitutional laws of the land you could be ignored, fined or imprisoned. Statute Courts can only hear Statute Laws because it is a lower form of law and they are not capable or allowed to hear anything else.

(3) Proof of Claim

Proceedings in a court of law, no matter what law is being practiced, rely on facts. That means something of substance, something physical like paperwork so always come prepared with plenty of evidence. That means all correspondence, receipts, invoices, contracts, claims and your affidavit of truth.

(4) Affidavit of Truth

This is a written sworn statement of fact voluntarily made by an affiant or deponent, under an oath or affirmation administered by a natural person authorised to do so by law, which means you. Such statement is witnessed as to the authenticity of the affiant's signature by a taker of oaths, such as a notary public or commissioner of oaths. The name is Medieval Latin for 'he has declared upon oath'. An affidavit is a type of verified statement or showing, or in other words, it contains verification, meaning it is under oath which carries the penalty of perjury, and this serves as evidence to its veracity and is required for court proceedings. Affidavits work because in law, they override everything else that comes before them. Affidavits offer the Facts, Harmony and maybe more importantly when it comes to law, the Agreement of the parties. The other good thing about an affidavit of truth is as they can only be made by a natural person; corporate entities are incapable of performing this duty.

Back to your artificial person, you might hear it being referred to as a Strawman or some other name but however named, it's your ticket to engage in commercial activity if you wish. You can enter into contracts, open bank accounts, get a loan or credit cards, get a mortgage, get employed, drive and "Traffic" (see legal definition). Traffic you say? Yes traffic. Traffic is commerce as opposed to a traffic jam, yes I know. I was just as surprised as you the first time I looked it up in a law dictionary. All of us "Driving" on the public roads are not aware that we are engaging in commerce, really. The correct term is "Travelling" and it is not "Passengers" that's in my car, those people they pay to travel, anyone in my car that is not paying for a service is known as a "Guest", this is for those operating in the private and not conducting business on the roads. If you are conducting business on the public roads then you must be regulated like any other form of commerce and be subject to Statute Laws hence Taxes, Certificates, Licences, Penalties, Charges etc. Or are you? What if you're conducting your own private business and need the public roads to get your goods and services around, what then? Well it all depends on what "Capacity" you were performing those "Duties" in. Were you the natural person, or were you acting in the capacity of the artificial person? If I were you I would always remain as the natural person and if anyone suggest otherwise they would have to provide proof to back up whatever their claiming, as they are the ones making the assumptions as to who and what you are, aren't they?

Bouvier's Law Dictionary

Person:

(1) This word is applied to men, women and children, who are called natural persons. In law, man and person are not exactly synonymous terms. Any human being is a man, whether he be a member of society or not, whatever may be the rank he holds, or whatever may be his age and sex. A person is a man considered according to the rank he holds in society, with all the rights to which the place he holds entitles him, and the duties which it imposes.

(2) It is also used to denote a corporation which is an artificial person.

Black's Law Dictionary

Traffic: Commerce; trade; dealings in merchandise, bills, money, and the like.

The Construct

Here's a good question to ask yourself; do you trust your government? Do you really? If your answer is yes then I think you're in a small percentage of people that feel that way, but if your answer is one you're unsure of then you can obviously see something that you're not too happy with, you know something is not right with the world presented before you. It is a feeling you get deep inside that things are not the way they're supposed to be. So you search for answers from the ones you put to lead you, but your questions always seem to be either ignored, diverted or received with hostility and ridicule. This leads many people down road of distrust of the government's explanations as to what is really going on with the country, and why. When people are treated with such disdain, faith diminishes along with trust and soon nothing that's said is believed anymore, this is where you begin to see everything differently. You know that uncanny feeling you get of wanting to slap a politician as soon as they open their mouth before all the drivel and lies fall out? Trust that! You can never lie to yourself even if you try.

The thing is you sense that something is wrong. What that something is you just can't explain because you don't know what it is exactly but you can feel it. You know there is just something terribly wrong with society and mankind was not meant to live like this. I'll give you an example of what I mean. It's 7am your alarm clock wakes you up, you hit the snooze button only to be woken up 10 minutes later, you roll grudgingly out of bed, jump in the shower, get dressed, skip breakfast because you're running late for work, sit in the traffic for an hour if you're lucky because you could have been standing at a bus stop or waiting on a train in the cold. You get to that job you don't even enjoy with people you could just about tolerate for the next 9 hours or so. You get a break for lunch but not long enough for a decent meal so every-day you just grab some fast food that is full of artificial and unhealthy crap. When you finish your day you travel back home in more traffic or by having to cram onto public transport with some guy's smelly armpit in your face only to get home eventually to a rubbish frozen meal because you're too tired to cook anything healthy. You then sit and watch mind numbing TV for a couple of hours before going to bed because its only Monday and you've got to do this for the rest of the week because you have bills that need paying if you want to live and be comfortable. But that's okay; at least you've got the weekends off to do all the crap you like to do anyway, brilliant! Come on! This is insanity made acceptable because if given an alternative I know which one I'd choose. There has got to be more to us and to life than just this? Wouldn't you agree?

The world around us is not as we believe it to be and if we were all to awaken to the corrupt system today, things would change overnight. This system of things that has been put into place I like to call "The Construct" simply because there are so many branches of system working together to make you the unsuspecting party none the wiser as to what's really going on, all the while gaining more and more control over every aspect of your life and freedom. After all, isn't it obvious to see these days that control is one of their main objectives? I'll keep mentioning 'they' and 'them', those who hide in the shadows pulling the strings of the leaders to carry out their own unscrupulous, secret agendas. The thing is we can all make assumptions as to who these people might be like say the Illuminati, the Free Masons, the Bilderberg Group, the Rockefeller's or Rothschild's who are the owners of our largest and most powerful banking institutions in the world, or maybe it's reptiles carrying out the orders of little grey men. We just don't have 100% proof. All we do know without a doubt is that someone or something is sitting on top of the pyramid of the food chain influencing all aspects of our economy, society and even our daily life. It's all part of the construct designed for a specific purpose, to get every man, woman and child from birth to accept the programs as normality, to abide by manmade laws, acts and statutes, to have the state school indoctrination and their version of history, converting young minds making them incapable of critical thinking, training you to become a mindless product of societies labour-force and eventually a never ending consumer who will not only be subjected to their exploitation but will believe it, engage with it as though it is normal and finally embrace it.

You are told from a young age that you need to pay attention in school and make sure you get a good education. Without one you won't be able to get a good job and earn a living because that's what's important in life. With that good job you'll earn good money because success is what it's all about, you will be able to afford things you want and people will look up to you. You will be able to purchase that big house and a sports car and you will be the envy of all your friends, even your parents will be boasting about you to their neighbours and friends and about how much money they have spent on your education and how proud they are of your achievements. I know what you're saying, what's wrong with ambition and wanting to become successful? Answer, nothing and also everything. You are participating in an illusion and until you understand that ideology only then you can see the harmful effects it has propagated against humankind. Don't get me wrong things were not meant to be like this. Somewhere down the line someone or a small group of individuals saw that they could profit from it all if they could basically take control of the system by keeping the rest of us in the dark and constantly living in fear, to become totally reliant on their leaders to come to their rescue at the first sign of trouble. Everything government does is supposed to be in our interest, by and for the people, working for the majority, who by the way seems to be on middle and low incomes, struggling to feed their families and pay the bills not the minority of multi millionaires that are always rubbing shoulders at dinner parties in 10 Downing Street or The White House. Can you honestly say that all these years government has existed has it ever worked efficiently, well for us hardworking folk anyway? Look at the state your country is in right now, besides the never ending wars the rich seem to keep getting richer and of course like the laws of physics the poor keep getting poorer.

This veil that has been draped over our eyes depends upon us accepting the programme; we must believe, participate and defend it whenever it's questioned. We must work, be a part of the system in order to live. You must now earn your entitlement to exist, living is not a right, a gift to experience as you please, your life can only be earned through hard work and perseverance, keeping your head down and following orders proficiently. This construct is relying on us to incorporate our lives in this open air prison we now call society regardless of whatever your dreams may be. If it's not a contributing factor, it's not an option you have. Some jobs and even laws are created not for your benefit but as a necessity in this equation of dependency and conformity, they serve no purpose to the world, morality nor humanity. Somewhere along the line money, greed and lust for power corrupted everything so the laws put in place that are meant to protect us now enslave us. So what we must now do is search for knowledge; read and research; learn how the system works so we may manoeuvre through the misinterpretation and misinformation of the laws to be able to enforce our rights because if we are ignorant of our rights then we obviously haven't got any. What we are told about the facts of life are indeed far from it. What government do is reaffirm the hidden agendas put in place which all leads to one purpose and that purpose is to restrict any progression of the consciousness, preventing us from being true to who we really are and instead we're becoming docile and submissive where they can harness every bit of our energy.

> "We were not born critical of existing society. This would seem to lead to a simple conclusion: that we all have an enormous responsibility to bring to the attention of others information they do not have, which has the potential of causing them to rethink long-held ideas."
> **Howard Zinn – The Progressive, 2005**

> "The control of events has been taken out of our hands...we have fallen into the mighty current of eternal principles-invisible forces-which are shaping and fashioning events as they wish, using us only as instruments to work out their own results in our national destiny."
> **Frederick Douglass, 1816**

Energy

What is energy? The answer is everything. Everything is energy and energy is everywhere. I believe that and so did Albert Einstein. He knew this hence the formula:

$E=mc^2$ Energy is equal to mass times the speed of light squared. I believe that we are one of the greatest sources of energy on this earth just by what we can achieve. I love movies, for me they are a means of escape; they can take an alternative view of the world and reality where someone's messages can be portrayed in their storytelling, almost as to inform their viewers indirectly of what might actually be going on around us. In this instance most of us have seen the movie The Matrix, like many other similar stories for instance Alice In Wonderland and The Wonderful Wizard Of Oz where there is a clear message within the story. In the Matrix, the population was literally used like batteries to harvest their energy to power the machines, all the while everyone on earth was asleep, in a coma like state, living out their life in a dream world that they believed to be real, totally unaware as to the reality of their enslavement. Doesn't it seem quite similar to the very world in which we live today? As for the sometimes misunderstood or overlooked esoteric message, one that seems clear as day to me now, one not of any physical bondage but an enslavement just the same, one where you're not even aware of your servitude, a mental slavery, one where you're bound to the laws of commerce, trapped in the illusion, the construct created by man, one which you cannot possibly experience what the real world is because you don't even know what it is.

In this modern day lifestyle our possessions seem to now possess us. We have become unwittingly unaware of our own reliance upon the appliances that serve us as an instrument of assistance. It has now become a must have necessity that dictates our very existence. We no longer require what we only need in life, it is not enough, we now obsess. We have become obligated to satisfying our wants of meaningless, inanimate objects. Today we strive for the best jobs with the big paycheques so we can buy the biggest and best of everything in order to feed our own ego, that's all. That we may feel better about ourselves somehow and be the envy of others, inevitably to become trapped in a vicious cycle of greed, false pride and selfishness. We have now fallen from grace and forgotten who we really are. We are no longer a master, a being of pure thought. We have become a mindless consumer, a slave to objects and to idols. Our possessions now define us, they give us status in society, and they attach a title to us. All the while society keeps reminding us that were not successful enough, not beautiful enough, and not trendy enough, judging us, and repetitively saying we're just not good enough unless we buy some more stuff, right? But it's all fake, it's all in the land of make believe; dreamt up in the corporate board room. Just for the sake of making bigger profits, that's all. It's nothing personal it's only good business.

We are mass and mass is energy, and physics will tell you that energy will only transform or convert it never expires, so what does that say about us? Everything we do, think, feel or say is a form of energy that reverberates throughout our universe, all mass is connected so we are all one, and this is who we really are. We are powerful beings of pure energy capable of anything. We just don't know it, we have only forgotten. Ask yourself this, when does an echo stop? When you cease to hear it or is it still going on and on but at a lower frequency that your ears just can't hear? So in the most basic of terms we have unconsciously by our own design enslaved ourselves by focusing all of our energy, all our thoughts, all our actions and all our emotions on things of no substance and importance. Our thoughts are no longer pure which are produced by our conscious mind. It is now advertisements and televised programming, images, fear, our own ignorance of the world and ourselves, media and our arrogance that do our thinking for us now, telling us who we are and who we should be, tricking us by triggering emotions in our subconscious mind with the use of subliminal and suggestive messages. We no longer know who we are, what we really need and what great things we can achieve in our lives, instead marketing strategies and advertising tell us what to think, how to think and what we should do and that is to constantly and forevermore consume.

Life is simple but it has been corrupted and complicated for selfish means. We were not meant to live in this chaos of financial dependency. You must understand it's all been manufactured, it's not real. Financial security is what most of us require, those of us who are plugged into the system because they're afraid of the consequences if they do not participate or are unable to find other solutions to maintain their lifestyles. I fully understand their concerns but alternatives are available for those who desire to truly live free. Could you just imagine if tomorrow most of the world snapped out of the hypnotic state it's in and stopped being selfish and greedy and fearful and angry, burden by worry and stress and instead just decided to say you know what, life's too short, let's focus all our energy on what's really important in this world. Look after each other, our families, our friends and respect each other and love each other. Soon enough I believe that love will echo throughout the universe and empower us all. Isn't that our true purpose? To love, live and be happy. Or is it our purpose to be successful, famous, wealthy and important? I've heard the saying there is no stronger power than the power of love, that love conquers all and you know what, I believe it.

> "Concerning matter, we have been all wrong. What we have called matter is energy, whose vibration has been so lowered as to be perceptible to the senses. There is no matter."
> **Albert Einstein**

> "If you want to find the secrets of the universe, think in terms of energy, frequency and vibration."
> **Nikola Tesla**

CHAPTER 2

What Is Real, Really?

The 5 Senses

What we perceive to be reality in this world and the universe is no more than information received from our entire body and transmitted as electric pulses to our brain which will be processed as touch, taste, smell, sight and sound. Without our senses conventional reality as we know it would cease to exist. Our five senses interpret things differently than we realise, when they are all examined, the evidence will show that it comes down to three things energy, frequency and vibration. This is what makes up our everyday reality which is also all matter and matter is made up of atom particles, it just depends on its density. What does all this mean? Well how can I put it? Everything is nothing (but particles) and nothing is everything. It is not perceived this way because maybe our brains have been desensitised or maybe it is due to our human devolution as to how we now interpret certain information.

It is said that the average person only uses about 5% of their brain. Imagine the possibilities if we could use 25% or even 50%. What effect would that have on the way we process information? Think about it.

The reason for all this scientific explanation is to show you that the way you perceive something, from the way your brain interprets that information is not as that thing really is. It's not our fault or our parents' it is just the way the world has been designed. We are taught everything from day one making it almost impossible to resist this sort of mental programming. Now it is our duty to set forth a curriculum for ourselves and our children and even our community so we can unlearn the mental blockades and become a conscious being again. One thing we can all agree on is no matter how someone brings up their children, somehow they always seem to have their very own personality no matter how strict an upbringing, but how can this be? Where does this come from, and why? Despite all of the teachings, all of the programming, all the influence, all the do's and don'ts, rights and wrongs, all the morals you instil, knowledge, education and beliefs etc. I am surprised that to this day still no two personalities are exactly the same. It seems that our personality doesn't just develop from information gathered by our senses instead it seems that our personality was already with us even before we were born and that's what makes us unique.

If we could carry out an experiment where we could suppress all of our senses somehow, what would we be left with? Let's see, if you were placed in a room with no light only complete darkness, also that room was able to cut off all sound, then say that room had some way to deprive you of smell, taste and feeling also. What do you think will happen in your mind? This practice is called Sensory Deprivation, but if we are deprived of all of our senses how or why does our mind still stay conscious? There must be something more, something else present and functioning than of just the five senses which we know. Consciousness is something that is still debated to this day as to what it is exactly. Some call it the sprit, the soul, the inner voice, the third eye, the chackra, the universe, energy etc. The truth is I haven't got a clue to what it is either, but what I do know, it is something that's very much there, something very real and it's there to guide me. That's why instead of calling this technique sensory deprivation I prefer to call it Amplified Consciousness, this is perhaps, I think our five senses now also work as more of a distraction for our inner mind so by suppressing them we allow our brain a road free of all traffic that it may be possible to concentrate all of our focus and connect with the world and even universe with the most powerful of all our senses, Consciousness. It is the sole purpose of Meditation, it has been used for centuries by many cultures for many various purposes like relaxation, build internal energy or life force (qi, ki, prana, etc.) and to develop compassion, love, patience, generosity and forgiveness, understanding, strength, enhance physical ability, relieve stress and in some instances even heal. These things lead me to believe it is real and the most powerful of all our senses, you can call it whatever you like but I call it our sixth sense.

> "Well, you see the people have a voice inside of them that talk to them, you know? That is the voice that these people must listen to. Because in everything you go and do, there is a wrong way and a right way, and if you listen good, you will know the right way. You know? Because, there's a voice inside talking to everyone."
>
> **Bob Marley**

> "It's clearly a crisis of two things: of consciousness and conditioning. We have the technological power, the engineering skills to save our planet, to cure disease, to feed the hungry, to end war; But we lack the intellectual vision, the ability to change our minds. We must decondition ourselves from 10,000 years of bad behaviour. And, it's not easy."
>
> **Terence McKenna**

The Sixth Sense

From a very young age I have always been full of questions, always searching for answers because the status quo never really sat well with me. You can call me a rebel, a sceptic, call me whatever you like. But if something seems a little bit fishy, a little bit unexplainable or just didn't make any sense to me I've got to question it, so I always trust and go by my instincts and it hasn't lead me astray so far. I grew up in a Christian dominated country with a Christian family background but I found it hard to conform to Christian Religious Traditions, when not even the Pope could explain general aspects of his belief, when the only answer for the lack of facts is, 'to just have faith my son'. I also struggled to cope with my secondary school curriculum, not that I had a problem with learning. I was always an "A" grade student but I became bored with just having to memorise stuff that probably wouldn't be of any relevance in any future career I may choose to pursue, although I did finish school I didn't spend much time there and the time I did I mostly remained in the art class drawing and reading.

There was also politics, something I take a keen interest in but to this day I have never got actively involved, by which I mean voting. I have never voted to this day and probably never will. I would listen to my parents over a period of years deliberate about their parties policies, about who had the countries best interest but regardless; whosoever was elected always failed the people nor live up to their promises in the end only to continue repeating the cycle of either their incompetency or blatant selfish interest deceiving the naive public again and again. These are just some examples of how I tend to rationalise things where I need things like facts, evidence, freedom of expression, imagination and good old common sense. In order to know something I need to fully understand it, only then can I believe it to be truth, then I can have faith in it. If something didn't feel right to me I had to find out why or I had to get to the bottom of it, I needed answers because it couldn't just be pushed to the back of my mind and become nonexistent to my reality, because eventually that something would burn a hole in my head. But why do we get that feeling that maybe something is not right? Why do we struggle to accept certain beliefs to be fact? What makes us question anything? Hey if we all believed everything we were told we would have never had sailed the seas because someone convinced us all back then that the earth was flat, right?

We are all born with what we refer to as instincts, some subconscious function of the mind that goes off like a siren on an emergency vehicle at the first smell of bullshit telling us 'you know what, don't accept this as gospel, you might actually need to look into this'. We need to seek the truth. It's only natural to be curious and inquisitive like a child that keeps asking why to every answer they're given. You must question everything and when you find an answer question it again. If you're just going to believe everything people say or always follow popular opinion, then what is the point of having instincts? They're there for a reason. It is only after you spend time reading and studying and researching something, only then you realize how much you really don't know anything at all.

By developing or enhancing what I refer to as our sixth sense, through meditation we allow a natural process of self knowledge. The thing is, without trying to sound like a Buddhist, I believe that all the answers we seek lies within. Let me explain what I'm getting at. When the Wright brothers came up with the idea to build a flying machine to actually be piloted by man across the sky, where did that ingenuity come from? There were no blueprints or models in existence so where could they have gotten their ideas from? No one showed them how to do it, or was it the Aliens? In fact everyone thought they were absolutely crazy and would eventually kill themselves. People said that it was impossible for man to fly, it cannot be done but they created it out of thought and from their thought came reality. Everything created, every car, every plane, every gun, every bomb, machine, television, radio, CD, camera; every invention first started off as a single thought in the mind. So I wonder, does that mean that anything my mind can conceive I can make it a reality? Change the way you look at the world and the world changes. That leads me back to you, your thoughts also define who you are. If any of your thoughts are negative, evil, greedy, envious, selfish, egotistic, angry, judgmental, spiteful or hateful what kind of person would you become? But if instead our thoughts were positive, pleasant, happy, helpful, caring, compassionate, forgiving, open minded and nothing but full of love, well then it becomes obvious as to what kind of person you will become, so need I say more?

"It always seems impossible until it's done."
Nelson Mandela

"If my mind can conceive it, and my heart can believe it - then I can achieve it."

"Impossible is just a big word thrown around by small men who find it easier to live in the world they've been given than to explore the power they have to change it. Impossible is not a fact. It's an opinion. Impossible is not a declaration. It's a dare. Impossible is potential. Impossible is temporary. Impossible is nothing."

Muhammad Ali

"Everything is theoretically impossible, until it is done."

Robert A. Heinlein

"If you always put limits on everything you do, physical or anything else, it will spread into your work and into your life. There are no limits. There are only plateaus, and you must not stay there, you must go beyond them."

"If you think a thing is impossible, you'll only make it impossible."

Bruce Lee

Family

When I ask people, what is the most important and most valued thing to them? Most if not everyone says their family, but why? Why not money, fame, or success, or longevity? Why is family so important to everyone? See, I think it's more than just gratitude, or passing on our genes, or the family name or title, or maybe just having someone there to wipe your butt when you get old. No, I didn't think so either, but it's so obvious if we really thought about it. We all have our own personal accomplishments that we all aspire to whether it's something simple like having a career that helps our community or something more like being very successful in society. Whatever the reasons may be it all comes back down to one thing, having someone to share it with, someone to love and to be loved by.

Love is the only answer I could come up with when looking into, and trying to understand the pursuit of our happiness. It's surely a good enough reason. No I'm positive it's definitely the best and only reason for everything, everything that really matters. It is our family and friends that make life worth living and enjoyable, what would we possibly do without them? Nobody really wants to be alone, live by themselves all their life and to die alone without ever experiencing love, well at least no one I know of. Unconditional Love is all we need for everyone and everything in this world including love of ourselves. If you're still wondering; what is the meaning of life? Why are we here?

And what is the purpose of our existence? Then you obviously haven't experienced love yet.

I know what you're saying but I do love myself. Do you? Really? To love yourself first you need to accept yourself for who you are because we are not perfect and we never will be. Look at your reflection in the mirror. Do you see anything you don't love? What about your personality, is there anything about it that troubles you? Do you feel that you may hold any prejudices towards anyone? Do you have any bad habits? These are the insecurities within us that we tend to divert towards other people in order to feel better of ourselves, judging others, passing on our warped views to our children and manifesting a breeding ground of contempt for future generations. The good thing is if we are honest and accept ourselves only then we can adjust our consciousness and start loving ourselves again. In turn it will empower us to let go of all our fears, anger, jealousy, pain and suffering that's being self inflicted so it may free us from our emotional and psychological bondage to be free to love everyone in the same manner. I know I say this as though it was the easiest thing to do when in fact it's probably the hardest thing to do, to conquer one's self and to master one's ego. The ego is a false version of you that compels our natural self to become an image, an idol to be accepted and glorified by everyone which is encouraged by and being propagated by society's corporate media. We must not feed the ego. It is only a persona, an act, it is not who you really are or meant to ever become. It is an imposter. I'm concerned by people that can can only envision the world through their narrow perception and one dimensional thinking. They believe success and their version of achievement, the one that society has formed to reward and idolise, where status, fame and wealth are applauded, titles and notability or even notoriety are desired because we have constructed this ideology around what is deemed important and beneficial to that society. This ego, a false byproduct of the conscious psyche which is a direct manifestation of the illusion, the human experience we call reality. It is not our true self, our true spiritual nature.

Just trying to resist submitting to your egotistic lust is a big enough step in the right direction. It takes a great deal of strength and willpower to overcome desires and temptations. Trust me this is a daily battle and you have got to keep reminding yourself of the journey you're on. It's a personal journey you must take to find your true self, because your true self is love. Your family and friends are also true love. Conquer the ego and you will achieve something beautiful and pure. Try taking some time out for yourself, disconnect, be a recluse for about ten minutes a day when it's quiet and just lie down, close your eyes and just reflect, focus and let your mind wander but pay close attention or concentrate on only what really matters. You might say it's a form of meditation or maybe it's just you gathering your thoughts or clearing your mind for the day I really can't say but just give it a try. Who knows you may connect with that little voice inside your head and out of the blue, just like that, the answers and strength you seek may come.

> "When the power of love overcomes the love of power, the world will know peace."
> **Jimi Hendrix**

> "The meaning of life is that it is to be lived, and it is not to be traded and conceptualized and squeezed into a pattern of systems."
> **Bruce Lee**

> "Love is life. All, everything that I understand, I understand only because I love. Everything is, everything exists, only because I love. Everything is united by it alone. Love is God,

and to die means that I, a particle of love, shall return to the general and eternal source."

Leo Tolstoy – War and Peace

"What can you do to promote world peace? Go home and love your family."

Mother Teresa

The Earth

The electrical resonance of the Earth lies between 6-8 Hz, some call this basic frequency the Earth's "heartbeat" or the "tuning fork" of the planet this coincides with alpha rhythms produced by the human brain during meditation, relaxation and creativity. The dominant brain wave rhythm of all mammals is the alpha or resting state also of 6-8 Hz. Hmm, coincidence? We all live on this one planet, all of us. This is our home, our only home. The Earth sustains all life that we presently know of, if the earth dies we die with it so why do we show such disdain for our world? It confuses me while trying to comprehend the logic as to what happens when we destroy the planet so much it becomes uninhabitable, what then? After all it has been here for millions of years and throughout this time it has gone through unimaginable transformations. It evolves and it will keep on evolving, with or without us.

To the ancients it was believed that the earth is a living organism that should be loved and cherished and treated with respect. It was also referred to as Mother Earth or Gaia as it was the giver of life. By just looking around and observing you can see that life sprouts from it, it also nurtures us the way a parent would a child by providing us with all we could ever need starting with the most basic of needs like food, clothing and shelter. We now seem to take our only home for granted, as something we can own, exploit and abuse as we see fit all for the sake of making profits. If we do not change our current way of life the Earth will eventually die or become unable to sustain life from all of the trauma inflicted upon it or maybe the Earth will fight back the only way it can with what we would deem to be natural disasters and attack the disease that's making it sick. I tend to believe the latter. When I was a lot younger I always heard about these people going around chaining themselves to trees while there would be other people hurling abuse at them calling them hippies and tree huggers telling them to go get a job and all sorts of degrading things. I then found myself thinking, why are they trying to save a few trees? What is all that about? Today I look at the world and I see mass deforestation changing landscapes permanently and evicting native civilisations from their ancestral land forever, without concern for any repercussions from the effects it may cause. The fact of the matter is that trees are integral to our survival, with the rapid decline we limit ourselves to their product of oxygen and the last time I checked, it's vital to us.

We also have an insatiable need for, and reliance on fossil fuels for energy; to drive our cars, heat our homes, electricity etc. and although some strive for alternative forms of energy that doesn't harm our planet, which seems to be here and available but we still demand greater oil supply as though clean energy was somehow not good enough, not efficient enough. It just won't make our cars go fast enough, even though by using it we could save our planet. But again where's the profit in that? It's just not very good for business, so we continue to burn fossil fuels with the drawback of polluting the air and water that every living thing on this planet needs to survive. Then there's nuclear energy not to mention nuclear weapons whose by product is nuclear waste. Great so not only are we killing ourselves we're now going to speed up the process. We are committing mass suicide on a global scale and because of our reluctance to take action in changing our lifestyles and seek alternative energy sources, we are only aiding the process toward destruction to materialise much sooner than later. Soon our seas and rivers, our soil and air will be so toxic there would be no fish in the ocean, no birds in the sky and all the animals and crops will start to wither away and eventually everything will die. All we would be left with is genetically modified foods; nothing pure and natural would be available to us anymore. I'm not trying to scare you but what we're facing is true. It's more of a rude awakening, bringing this importance to your attention so you may see things as I now do. Our world is nothing more than a speck in the vastness of the universe but this speck is our only home, our entire world and yet this speck is a part of the vast universe.

As we now know the problem we face we can start to work towards a solution. We need balance and harmony with the eco-system. The earth belongs to all of us, it's all of our responsibility. We are all human beings living here and must share it equally but some people don't think that's a good idea somehow they believe that they deserve a greater claim to the planet and its resources than anyone else. They would rather separate and segregate nations from nations, call their people citizens and others foreigners and aliens, divide the land and wealth amongst themselves and put up borders, restrict free movement and free enterprise, impose embargoes and sanctions while exploiting less developed nations for their own selfish agendas. If we don't all work together soon we the human race won't make it. We will either destroy the Earth to such a degree that it will be impossible to even breathe, or the Earth will in turn destroy us. Our leaders are not working in our best interest. Making money by being competitive in the global market seems to be top of the list. I'm no eco-warrior believe me. I'm not. I don't even recycle but I get it. I now understand what the hippies and tree huggers' fight is all about. This is my home, my family's home, my only home and it's yours too. If someone came to your house where you and your family lived and walked in with their muddy boots on your carpet, lit up a cigarette in front of your children, dropped their beer can and food wrappers on your floor and then after all that they decided they liked your beautiful house so much they took it from you, abused it until it was destroyed by burning it to the ground, I'm guessing you're going to have something very strong to say about that, right?

> "There manifests itself in the fully developed being, Man, a desire mysterious, inscrutable and irresistible: to imitate nature, to create, to work himself the wonders he perceives. Long ago he recognized that all perceptible matter comes from a primary substance, or tenuity beyond conception, filling all space, the Akasa or luminiferous ether, which is acted upon by the life giving Prana or creative force, calling into existence, in never ending cycles all things and phenomena. The primary substance, thrown into infinitesimal whirls of prodigious velocity, becomes gross matter; the force subsiding, the motion ceases and matter disappears, reverting to the primary substance."
> **Nikola Tesla, 1908**

> "This planet is for everyone, borders are for no one. It's all about freedom."
> **Benjamin Zephaniah – Refugee Boy**

Chapter 3

Things We Say & Do

Everyday Language

In today's society our language is open to vast interpretations. New words arise while meanings of words we use often get lost, used out of context and sometimes meanings even change entirely. What this does is mislead, confuse, deter and refrain anyone from trying to seek knowledge, process and understand information while trying to educate themselves and their family. We are all guilty of doing this not realising the power and influence words have, especially when the so-called authorised books which is supposed to be there to guide us gives us a biased slant on their meaning. We use negative words and interpret them as positive and vice versa not realising the effects they may have over someone and their ability to fully understand what they were really intended for and their associations.

Some of the main perpetrators engaged in propagating this distortion of definitions on a global scale is the mainstream media i.e. news corporations, press, advertising, television programs, film and music industry and especially governments. I'll give you a simple example.

It is now common practice, accepted globally to refer and identify a race of people with colours like black and white, although there is no country or tribe known with that name. Nonetheless, it is now institutionally accepted as the norm. Obviously it's used as being descriptive and that would be ok if words were not open to so many different interpretations. What this does is to subconsciously attach a stigma to one while glorifying the next i.e. the word Black when used in association with other words becomes negative in nature like black magic, black listed, black heart, black thoughts, black looks, also saying the future looks black, and Black Friday can now make a day become cursed. Other demeaning words are attributed to black i.e. evil, wicked, dark, soiled, angry, hostility, hopeless, sinister, bleak and many more. What is left for a young mind to perceive when called black, is he not to believe he is nothing more than something negative? On the other hand the word White when used in association with other words becomes positive i.e. white magic, white knight, white witch, white wizard, even a white lie becomes something that can now be tolerated and can be for your benefit. Then just like black, the word white in comparison has other words attributed to it as well which all seem totally benevolent i.e. pure, clean, innocent, good, immaculate, unblemished, sinless etc. so now I guess you get the picture. Words are more than just descriptions of things. They empower and exalt or degrade and destroy so be careful what you call yourself and others.

History would tell us in this instance that a race of people are either European if from Europe or African if from the continent of Africa but I prefer to call them Native people of the land. Native or Original people of the land known today as Australia are given a name of Aboriginal. It's a name I will always have problems accepting with ab- being put in front of the word -original. Surely that should mean Not Original, right? As in Normal and Abnormal. Shouldn't we question as to what the natives might have called themselves before giving them that identity? The same was done with Native Americans calling them Indians but as we know India is on a different continent entirely. This pertains to all people of all demographical origins, this is just one example. Once we look into their history we see evidence of this taking place, but why? Another is the redefining of meanings. You will find that a dictionary from a century ago would have its words redefined in today's copies but why would we need to change or add different definitions to a word?

A word is something descriptive, it gives meaning, authority, and power and in turn, control. Control of your thoughts. If you control the meanings, the very definitions of words, you control the collective thoughts of society. Words and images evoke thoughts and in turn they determine our emotions and feelings thereby controlling our actions. So those that control the definitions, the way words are used and in what context their used can control the way we think hence control what we do. It's the main driving force behind the reason for what we say, buy, eat, learn, live, wear, drive, vote and even perceive ourselves but more importantly others. Well at least on TV they call them programmes.

> "The basic tool for the manipulation of reality is the manipulation of words. If you can control the meaning of words, you can control the people who must use them."
> **Philip K. Dick**

> "The gift of words is the gift of deception and illusion."
> **Frank Herbert – Children of Dune**

> "But if thought corrupts language, language can also corrupt thought."
> **George Orwell, 1984**

Recreating Reality

"We seldom realize, for example that our most private thoughts and emotions are not actually our own. For we think in terms of languages and images which we did not invent, but which were given to us by our society."
Alan Wilson Watts

"The beginning of wisdom is the definition of terms."
Socrates

Why We Do the Things We Do

We make choices every day, but do we really make them for ourselves, or have our choices already been made for us before we even know? I mean what compels us to do certain things like buy a particular brand of dish washing liquid, or jeans or mobile phone? Why do we shop at particular popular outlets and supermarkets, are their prices any cheaper, their vegetables any fresher, or is it that you just like the way the isles are constructed, or maybe it's that check-out clerk you've got your eyes on? What makes us act a particular way, to automatically decide our choice of attire, our hairstyle, makeup or jewellery, what really influences us to make those choices? Is there even a choice to be made? If there is, do we make that choice, or has that choice already been planted in our brain even before we knew we wanted to eat baked beans with our eggs and toast this morning? It would seem that society already has an idea of what is deemed to be an acceptable type of behaviour and image which has been preconceived to be projected upon the public by every aspect of media available, constantly telling us that your life and everything about you sucks.

We've all been to the supermarket to buy our baked beans and without having to put much thought into it we went straight for the brand name tin, but why? Well it's the best of course, isn't it? Well it's certainly not the cheapest that's for sure so it must be the best tasting or maybe it's the pretty packaging, right? Well to be truthful we never even tried the other brands have we so how can we have made this choice without making a comparison with another? This informative and critical kind of thinking seems irrational and dangerous to corporate agendas because big profits can only be achieved by getting the majority on board and to do that they had to use means of manipulation. It has destroyed your individualism. Everything about you has now been manufactured upon what someone else's idea of you should be. Your choices which you think you make have all been created then implanted into your subconscious for you. When you link a thing, a product to a person's emotions, their inert instincts and feelings, the very thing that makes them feel liberated, special, important, powerful, attractive, envied, sexy etc. then how can you possibly even have the slightest chance at making an informed and educated decision about anything at all?

Our senses are bombarded every waking moment of our lives from the advertisements being launched at us like ballistic missiles being fired from everywhere possible just to make sure we stick to the program. In the home there are adverts on the TV and radio, in the press and magazines, all carrying out their assault on home soil. As we take two steps outside our homes more adverts on cars, buses, bus-stops, trains, billboards, shops and even our own clothes with prints and symbols flashing like a great neon sign on our chest, head and feet. Its true we all like to look the best we can, dress in designer clothes, in the latest footwear, would like to drive a nice car and these days it's the newest technology we crave, even if the new and fancier gadget comes out and our present device still works perfectly we still want it because the one we now have is outdated. It's not trendy anymore. But what makes us think like this, buy things we don't need or even just buy certain products and brands? How do the corporations know what we want or even what's best for us before we do? Or do they manipulate us into wanting to buy their stuff?

What if they implant in our subconscious the idea that we need their product to feel happy, satisfied, confident, that we couldn't function without it? What if they somehow link having their product with our emotions, about how we feel about ourselves, playing on our insecurities telling us we're merely nothing without it, we're nobody and only when we purchase their product can we be what we desire to be, and others will desire us in-turn. So we just follow the crowd like sheep oblivious to the systematic corporate brain training, becoming efficient consumers. Ask yourself the next time the latest phone comes on the market, why do you really want it? Or more importantly do you really need it? I have, and the response from most people is, "I just want it". What? That's not even a reason! We don't know why we want their crap and we can't explain it. We've just got to have the latest accessory as though it was crack or heroin; we've just got to have it now!

Well it's all in part to a man called Edward Bernays. He was an Austrian-American pioneer in the field of public relations or more commonly known as propaganda, as referred to in his obituary as "the father of public relations". What he did was combined the ideas of Gustave Le Bon and Wilfred Trotter on crowd psychology with the psychoanalytical ideas of his uncle, Sigmund Freud for the benefit of commerce in order to promote, by indirection, an array of commodities. One of Bernays's favorite techniques for manipulating public opinion was the indirect use of third party authorities to plead his clients' causes. He would use an individual's psychic and emotional energy associated with instinctual biological drives, harness it and channel it toward corporate elite for economic benefit, great guy huh? Bernays writes in Manipulating Public Opinion (1928),

> "This is an age of mass production. In the mass production of materials a broad technique has been developed and applied to their distribution. In this age, too, there must be a technique for the mass distribution of ideas."

Bernays did eventually recognize the potential danger in so grand a scheme of his and in "This Business of Propaganda" He writes of the great caveat to his vision, a public relations counsel:

> "must never accept a retainer or assume a position which puts his duty to the groups he represents above his duty to society".

He realised the power of his methods to promote products of questionable value to humanity such as one of his greatest accomplishments, the cigarettes publicity campaign (1920) helping the tobacco industry, where he got women to smoke publicly at a time when it was a social taboo which he regretted later in life, after his wife died of lung cancer.

> "If you can influence the leaders, either with or without their conscious cooperation, you automatically influence the group which they sway".
>
> **Edward Bernays - Propaganda**

> "You want to reclaim your mind and get it out of the hands of the cultural engineers who want to turn you into a half-baked moron consuming all this trash that's being manufactured out of the bones of a dying world."
>
> **Terence McKenna**

> "If those in charge of our society - politicians, corporate executives, and owners of press and television - can dominate our ideas, they will be secure in their power. They will not need soldiers patrolling the streets. We will control ourselves."
>
> **Howard Zinn**

Insanity

It is truly amazing how far the human race has come in such a short period of time, but what can we say is man's greatest ever achievement? We have accomplished so much in medicine, technology, physics, science, construction etc. that we now venture into space, exploring alien worlds, take on massive scientific experiments like CERN with its Large Hadron Collider, committed to understanding how everything all began in the universe. We've constructed breathtaking buildings that touch the clouds, planes that smash the sound barrier which can also land on ships at sea. We have organised world events building stadiums, racetracks and state of the art indoor arenas all for the sake of entertainment. Then there is the military industrial complex, producing weapons of mass destruction, more than enough weapons that could destroy this planet a hundred times over, costing billions to the taxpayers every year, I ask why? Is that what we the people set out to achieve? We have created a world that once was thought to be unthinkable, now it's a dangerous place precariously balanced on the edge of oblivion. Another problem I have with all of this is the massive cost financially, morally and to our humanity but that won't stop the governments and mega rich corporations trying to justify and convince us of the important reasons for doing this, I guess they try to claim it's in our best interest, but somehow I seriously doubt it.

Don't get me wrong I'm all for the advancement of the human race but with the obscene amount of debt being mounted up by our government on defence, war and space exploration to name a few, while cutting public spending on healthcare, education and benefits to the poor and disabled makes me question their motives. Is this really all being done in the interest of the people or is it in the interest of the political and corporate agendas? There is also an issue of people living in absolute poverty, homeless, sick, some right here living amongst us, others in undeveloped countries dying of hunger and being exploited, being denied basic needs like access to clean water and food to feed their family although most of these countries are rich in natural resources which are being extracted by private corporations. Again I ask, what is going on? We can eradicate poverty overnight considering the obscene amounts of money being spent on war and defence alone. It's time to wake up and decide what is most important to us, fighting wars in someone's else's country and building more weapons or solving the poverty crisis and achieving peace? This should be our first priority, anything else should come after feeding people of the world but if I had to replace it with something else that could take the number one spot it would be peace. Am I being unreasonable? Or is it because there's no money to be made from peace? War is waged on countries overseas killing hundreds of thousands of innocent men, women and even children from little or no provocation or real imminent threat to us at all, while your government try to convince you the public that they are defending your freedoms by attacking first. But I wonder, in the end, who is it that profits from all this war?

Is this the world we have accepted to be reality. Where is our humanity, our love for others, our empathy? Have we become so desensitized to world occurrences that we no longer feel the pain and suffering of our fellow human beings? Are we that brainwashed by patriotic duty and allegiance to the flag that we celebrate the annihilation of a race of people that posed no threat to us and label the deaths of innocence as collateral damage? Where have our morals gone? We turn a blind eye to tyranny and oppression, inequality and injustice and carry on our daily lives watching it all unfold in front our eyes and feel totally unaffected. We are too distracted with our own lives, caught up watching our favourite reality TV shows, attend our sports matches, having our nights out at the bars, over indulging at meal time or maybe we are too stressed out to notice because of the bills that are now due. Could it be that pay rise you didn't get, rising cost of living on a fixed income or not having a job at all and just about getting by on benefits, but we still carry on fully knowing that our governments compete and destroy others just for the sake of profit, yes profit. It's that filthy little word the world loves so much so we may keep chasing the life we obsess on having, are we ok with that?

It's time for us to take a stand. We are better than this. We need to show compassion to the entire human race because every life is precious. We also need to exercise our power by making a stand against corporations and policy makers that hurt people and the environment. We can make them take notice by non participation in their commodities and their campaigns. If we stop buying into their crap they won't make money it's that simple, because that's all they care about in the end. If we hit them where it hurts the most, in their pocket then I guarantee they'll listen to us and change direction. I'm not asking you to go off like some superhero trying to save the world, all I'm asking is to try every now and then to do a simple act of divestment, stop giving away your earnings needlessly to these criminals and instead participate in an act kindness. There are hungry people in your own country, homeless, poor, disabled, orphaned, elderly, show them some compassion, love, some interest. A little generosity goes a long way, it comforts the soul. Trust me it feels right, you'll be a better person for it and if we all started doing it, caring for each other soon all the social ills in society can disappear forever. We have got to connect with each other again. We all possess the power to become a great people but we have to do it together, we have to get rid of the illusion that has been presented before us and stop competing with each other because no one is better than, nor does anyone deserve more than anyone else, anywhere.

The only way we will ever survive this great betrayal of our true identity and break free from our hypnotic state of materialism, fear, greed and anger is to understand we are all one. To harm someone is to harm ourselves, though we may not directly cause ourselves harm in the process, we diminish our integrity and our morality. Every action must have an equal and opposite reaction. It's physics you might say. Therefore everything we send out into this world, this universe comes right round back to us, you could say what goes around comes around, karma if you will. We have created this mess by subconsciously and by tacitly going along with the unjustified, unfair and unscrupulous actions of the ones that we put in charge and it is only us that can fix this problem so let's get started by changing the way we treat each other, work together and reclaim our humanity, our world and our sanity, don't you agree? In the end what is really most important, what can be our greatest achievement, is it not peace, is it not preserving mankind? If we fail to act and they continue abusing and wasting our resources, money, energy, technology, science and time on the things that they say are best for the country i.e. Space Exploration and not for the benefit of the people and the earth, then what's the point. I guess we should just let them get on with their search for another planet that can sustain life because this one won't be able to eventually.

> "Our society is run by insane people for insane objectives. I think we're being run by maniacs for maniacal ends and I think I'm liable to be put away as insane for expressing that. That's what's insane about it."
>
> **John Lennon**

"The greatest crimes in the world are not committed by people breaking the rules but by people following the rules. It's people who follow orders that drop bombs and massacre villages"

Banksy

"How wonderful it is that nobody need wait a single moment before starting to improve the world."

Anne Frank

"Simplicity, patience, compassion. These three are your greatest treasures. Simple in actions and thoughts, you return to the source of being. Patient with both friends and enemies, you accord with the way things are. Compassionate toward yourself, you reconcile all beings in the world."

Lao Tzu

Chapter 4

Law

Maritime Admiralty Law

There are two types of law. There is the Natural Law, which is a basic but fundamental law to our very existence, don't cause harm or loss to anyone or their property and to basically act responsibly and be accountable for all your actions. Everyone is subjected to this law as it comes naturally; we were born with these instinctive attributes. This law covers everything although we are expected to naturally act humane with our fellow man. Then there is all the other bullshit which is called law but are not Laws unless you give your consent to them. These are called Statute Law, or Acts, Bills and Codes which are more like what I refer to as rules of commerce. There are thousands of these so called laws and more being written into the books every week, so how are we supposed to abide by them if we don't even know them all and how could we? Hey, were screwed either way because ignorance of the law is no excuse as I'm sure you've heard before, but more importantly who do these laws govern, us? Or does it? If there is one thing I like doing whenever researching anything is to go back to the origins, so let's go back a bit and see where Maritime Admiralty Law originated.

Back in the early days of continental trade, the import and export of all maritime activities had to be maintained so maritime admiralty law which has now been incorporated as private international law, governed the relationships between private entities which operate vessels on the oceans. It dealt with matters including marine commerce, marine navigation, shipping, sailors, and the transportation of passengers and goods by sea. Admiralty law also covered many commercial activities even though it was land based or occurring wholly on land, as long as it was maritime in character it would fall under that jurisdiction. So simply it was the law of the seas put in place to regulate commerce, that's it. Later on it was introduced into England by the French Queen Eleanor of Aquitaine. Now special admiralty courts handle all admiralty cases, these courts do not use the common law of England, but are civil law courts largely based upon the Corpus Juris Civilis of Justinian. So once again don't go into one of these courts to enforce common law because you will be in the wrong jurisdiction and everything you say and do will be ignored by the judge and you will lose your claim leading to being fined or imprisoned or both. Henry De Bracton was an English jurist and famous for his writings on law in England who noted that admiralty law was also used as an alternative to the common law in Norman England. This previously required voluntary submission to it by entering a plea seeking judgment from the court. So you do not have to consent to admiralty law, you can refuse, decline or if you so choose you can conditionally accept but we'll talk about that in another chapter.

Maritime Admiralty Laws governs everything "Legal" and not "Lawful" and it works on assumptions. What I mean is it assumes you are operating within its jurisdiction at all times. It acts as though you are carrying out some form of commerce and/or a function of government at every single moment because you're seen as a corporate entity, a "Person" as far as they are concerned so their laws can always apply to you. But of course this is not true. You are doing neither, even if you are a public servant I'm sure you already pay your taxes, too much if you ask me so whenever you're off duty you become a private entity again so any interactions with the police, state, council, crown or any corporate entity needs your consent. It is in your interest to correct this mistake because that is all that is happening here. They're making a mistake and assuming you are engaging in commerce. It is your duty, your responsibility, you must make it your job to inform them (the bastards) that you are operating in the private and you totally reject their offer to contract. Just say no thanks, it's that simple. If they persist and they will because of their ignorance of the law in fact ignorance of all laws, then you now have options it just depends on your situation or how you prefer to deal with it, for instance like a parking ticket and on the spot fines and charges remember "all men are innocent until proven guilty" or what would be the point of having courts and the legal process. Think about it? It's pointless trying to explain yourself to the police at the side of the road when they pull you over or the parking attendant, about that P.C.N. they just stuck to your car or property. They are just following orders, it's a job, and they are just doing what they were trained to do. They are not educated about laws, they are trained like you would your dog to sit, roll over and do his business outside. You don't explain your reasons to the dog, do you?

Try this the next time you get pulled over by the police for some alleged traffic violation if you're feeling bored, ask the person in the uniform if they know the "Legal" definition of "Traffic", that same Traffic Act they're trying to enforce upon you and you will see how ignorant of the law they really are. Don't get me wrong I'm not against the police they are not all bad, most of them do a great job fighting crime, protecting and serving the public so I've got a great deal of respect for some of them but for the bullies that won't even let you explain yourself, have no sense of reason, want to infringe on your inalienable human rights, forgot they are public servants and just out to abuse their fictitious power, those I will have my day in court with. When you stop being a public servant and become a corporate agent, a servant for collecting revenue from the general public, I have a big problem with that. So one of the best ways I believe is to learn all the rules so you can play their game and win. That way there is no misunderstanding when you make them pay severely, through the process of contracting.

> "We hold these truths to be self-evident, that all men are created equal, that they are endowed by their Creator with certain unalienable Rights, that among these are Life, Liberty and the pursuit of Happiness. That to secure these rights, Governments are instituted among Men, deriving their just powers from the consent of the governed, That whenever any Form of Government becomes destructive of these ends, it is the Right of the People to alter or to abolish it, and to institute new Government, laying its foundation on such principles and organizing its powers in such form, as to them shall seem most likely to affect their Safety and Happiness."
>
> **Thomas Jefferson**
> *The Declaration of Independence*

> "Law is often but the tyrant's will, and always so when it violates the right of an individual."
>
> **Thomas Jefferson**

> "One has a moral responsibility to disobey unjust laws."
>
> **Martin Luther King Jr**

Courts & Legalese

I have to admit I do enjoy getting a summons from the so-called Crown Court which is nothing more than a De Facto Court operating under the Crown Corporation. Yes another great deception of facts to trick you to believe you are a criminal; committing crimes against humanity when in fact you are just being punished by them relinquishing you of great sums of your hard earned money for being ignorant of the law. Everything we participate in, every interaction and even everywhere we live, without our knowledge, we are engaging in commerce by design. It's not because we want to. If we were given the option we would tell them exactly where they could poke it, that's why its hidden from us. In order for this trickery to be successful it needs our unwitting compliance. This is deception by fraud as I was once accused of myself by the corporate revenue collectors who refer to themselves as the police service.

The reason for the courts is to settle disputes by balancing the books of accounting. Remember, we are dealing in Maritime Admiralty Law so the judge is only interested in commercial activities bound by statutes, acts and codes. When we are "Summoned" before a court we must "Appear" to answer for some "Damage" we may have caused which is defined as "loss, injury, or deterioration, caused by the negligence, design, or accident of one person to another." Remember all these words are legal definitions and "Person" also means corporations, "Loss", "Injury" and "Deterioration" does not necessarily mean physical damage which can also be done to a natural person, it gives us the impression that we committed a "Crime." It is another way they prevent us from being competent enough to enforce our rights. If we cannot understand or speak the language used in the courtrooms how can we have any chance? This form of gibberish is the language of the law society which is called Legalese. If we all understood law there would not be a requirement for lawyers and they would all be off somewhere studying politics instead. These jokers are not there for your interest at all, I'm sorry to say. They are only interested in getting paid or why wouldn't we be taught this in school from a young age. It just seems logical, if it's something we all need to know why not teach it in school and why do they keep redefining legal definitions, how many more new editions of law dictionaries do we need? We are well within our rights to represent ourselves. The truth is they make it as difficult and confusing as possible to keep us in the dark as to what's really going on, enslavement. "Reading! No slave of mine is allowed to read!" Excerpt from the movie Mandingo.

Instead of empowering us with the knowledge we need from birth to be free they designed the world in such a very clever way that it's hidden from us through misinformation and distractions that we may not only participate in our own mental enslavement but anyone or any attempt to emancipate us from our chains is seen as a threat, an enemy to the illusions of our security, justice and free will of this society. The scales of justice is weighted heavily on the side of corporations considering we enter the arena of the courts underprepared with the little knowledge of self, law and procedures. It is the reason why we seldom win and take great pride in victory when we do by some technicality when in fact were not meant to be there in the first place and I would not recommend it either unless you're making a claim against another "Person", but if you do decide to "Appear" in court on some crap statute violation we must first know a few things:

(1) In what "Capacity" are you appearing?

This is very important to know because it will decide if their so-called statutes have any "Authority" over you or not. Not that they do but you should always appear as the "Natural Person" with inalienable rights given by the creator, subject only to natural law and not the "Artificial Person" who's "Subject" to and given certain benefits and privileges by government which they can abuse as they see fit. Well I know which one I'd choose.

(2) Evidence

Never walk into court with your two arms swinging. Make sure you got a stack of paperwork to prove everything you're claiming by following a lawful process i.e. All Correspondence, Receipts, Tacit Agreements and Affidavit of Truth. These things will help make an "Affirmation" without a reasonable doubt that you are innocent of all claims and/or charges also that you tried to settle any financial obligations with your adversary lawfully by acting honourably.

(3) Agree with Thy Adversary, but, not really

This is where you put the responsibility of providing "Proof Of Claim" unto your accuser. This is called Conditional Acceptance. Why must you be required to provide any evidence for your defence at all if the prosecution can't prove to the courts that you are within their "Jurisdiction", what do I mean? If their phoney laws apply to you then you must either be involved in commerce and/or carrying out a form of government so let them provide proof of that in some form of contract, receipt, pay slip, job order, certificate, licence or invoice otherwise, your honour if the prosecution has no evidence to back up their claim, well then I motion to quash, you've obviously got the wrong man. But hang on, wait a minute, these are false claims that have been made against me and caused my family and I harm and distress, damaging my good reputation, leaving me no option but to seek "Remedy".

Black's Law Dictionary

Authority: In contracts. The lawful delegation of power by one person to another.

Subject: That concerning which the affirmation in a proposition is made; the first word in a proposition. An individual matter considered as the object of legislation.

Legal Capacity: is the attribute of a person who can acquire new rights, or transfer rights, or assume duties, according to the mere dictates of his own will, as manifested in juristic acts, without any restraint or hindrance arising from his status or legal condition.

Remedy: is the means by which the violation of a right is prevented, redressed, or compensated.

Conditional Acceptance

When there is a civil claim or financial dispute between two parties, whether it's the bank, debt collectors, a person or any corporate entity where they claim you owe any sum of money to them and you say that you don't, what you have now created is what's called "Controversy". When this happens in Maritime Admiralty Law disputes of this nature it is settled in court by a mediator, the judge who will consider all the facts presented before them so they can past judgement in favour of whosoever provides sufficient evidence of their claim in order to settle the account. One way to first deal with such matters is;

(1) By Way Of Direct Discussion

Even if the claim goes to court you can still write to the court manager to inform them of your intention to perform this and the courts can actually back off and let you get on with it. If this fails and it probably will because the claimant has already logged a claim with the courts and also believes they have a valid claim to get judgement it would most likely result with them ignoring your request but there are other options. Although most people just cave into submission once they receive a summons, what you do next is agree with your adversary but with conditions, known as:

(2) Conditional Acceptance

What this does is remove all controversy hence taking away the courts involvement in the matter. If you agree with the claimant to pay their claim in full then the matter is seen as settled and there is no need for a mediator but you also agree on the condition that they provide you with some evidence in the form of documents which is their "Proof Of Claim" if you are required to lawfully pay them anything. By doing this you eliminate the need for court proceedings the judge will not get involved in the matter because how can they now? Imagine the claimant going to file a claim telling the court that you're going to pay them in full only if they provide you with their proof of claim, a contract. Think of how ridiculous they would sound? They'll probably be laughed at, right out of the building because how can they make a case of someone agreeing with them? All you're doing is keeping in stipulation with contract law, yes you're just following the rules set in stone under these same laws. It's well within your rights to ask for proof of claim or how else can you know if you're dealing with the right corporate entity, owing them. After all they could be any old Joe demanding money from poor, naive, little old you.

(3) Capacity

Who is the claimant dealing with? Is it you the Natural Person, or you, the Artificial Person? This is another thing they will have to provide evidence for, especially if they're claiming you are the latter, which they will always assume you are. Why? Because that's the only entity they can contract with, so my advice is to always remain as the Natural Person that way there is no confusion as to who they are dealing with. So when you are in contact with your claimant or any corporate entity claiming anything from you, you always inform them to address you as John: Doe which is saying you are John of the Doe family, or clan, or tribe, you get the drift. Remember John Doe or Mr John Doe or Mr JOHN DOE or any variation of your name is an artificial title which they will try to get you to agree to being, this is where you get your affidavit of truth prepared by getting it notarised and included into your court records to be presented to the judge so your statements cannot be overlooked or ignored. When you conduct interactions with anyone natural or artificial, one thing you must always do is act honourably. Never intentionally go around doing things that you may benefit from financially, you will be defeating the point. It is the entire purpose of doing what's lawful and right in this world. The last thing you should ever consider doing is using your knowledge to get out of your responsibilities it is the whole purpose of Natural Law, to be responsible for your actions and amend them where you've caused harm or loss. Only when the corporate greed tries to drain you of your hard earned cash which is for you and your families benefit and well being while trying to enslave you in the world of commerce, I suggest you fight back. Making sure that all your correspondence is sent by recorded delivery and keep copies of everything just in case their only defence is to claim that they never received your letters in the first place, as I said you need as much evidence when it comes to matters in court to show who holds the better hand in this game.

> "A society whose citizens refuse to see and investigate the facts, who refuse to believe that their government and their media will routinely lie to them and fabricate a reality contrary to verifiable facts, is a society that chooses and deserves the Police State Dictatorship it's going to get."
> **Ian Williams Goddard**

> "The smart way to keep people passive and obedient is to strictly limit the spectrum of acceptable opinion, but allow very lively debate within that spectrum - even encourage

the more critical and dissident views. That gives people the sense that there's free thinking going on, while all the time the presuppositions of the system are being reinforced by the limits put on the range of the debate."

Noam Chomsky – The Common Good

"There is a higher law than the law of government. That's the law of conscience."

Kwame Ture

Contracting

When we hear the word contracts, we usually think in terms of signing on the dotted line, a document, a piece of paper with terms and conditions we must agree to, right? Well contracts are a lot more than something we sign just because we want a form of service performed for our benefit. No it is an "Agreement" between two or more "Persons" upon sufficient "Consideration" to do or not to do a particular thing.

Whenever you see this word "Consideration" in any document be very weary, it is not asking you to consider in the conventional sense, in law it's asking you to contract. So any letter with this word must be replied to by refusing and rejecting any and all offers. If you don't and ignore it you'll be saying yes by your silence and this is called "Acquiescence". Most contracts are between two persons, these are called bilateral contracts. Once entered into a bilateral contract the two parties are lawfully bound to it by contract law and no other. A third party may enter this agreement without express permission of both persons contracted. A simple example of persons using this assumptive contracting is Debt Collectors.

Once an agreement of the parties is met by way of a benefit, obviously for them both and everyone contracted is happy, which can be by way of negotiation this is called "a meeting of the minds", the contract then must be signed by both parties involved for it to become a legally binding document. If for some reason only one person in the agreement signs the contract then it remains null and void and it cannot be enforced by law.

Ok, let's say you pop into your bank to apply for a loan and the loan officer brings the loan agreement for you to sign, now if you read the contract (which we never do anyway) and there was something in there that we didn't agree with, let's say for example and this is only one example, we had to pay back interest of a thousand percent. It is well within our right to negotiate these terms. Oh yes! You can demand a lower rate of interest and you'll probably get it but we never do because when we apply (or should I say beg, because that's what they make us believe we're doing), we never consider the fact that contracts are always negotiable, always. If we do not agree with any of the terms and conditions fully and out of shear desperation we sign the contract it is deemed as signing under duress also if it's signed by us forcefully, unknowingly, by trickery or by not understanding any of it fully (full disclosure) it then also becomes null and void.

Now you have defaulted on your loan and the debt collectors are after you, but why is it not the bank, after all was it not them you had the agreement with? How could the debt collectors have any authority to collect anything from you? Well they don't, none whatsoever, lawfully. They can't demand you to pay them anything. I know what you're thinking; they always threaten and demand as though they do, see this is all part of their deception. Your contract is bilateral which means it is between you and the bank and no one else, so for the bank to bring a third party into this agreement without your say so is not permitted. Debt collectors have no contract with you hence no power, never confirm anything to them especially by phone not even your name and if they persist just remind them of the Harassment Act 1997 and the Administration of Justice Act 1970, which makes it a criminal offence for a creditor or a creditor's agent to make demands (for money), which are aimed at causing alarm, distress or humiliation, because of their frequency or manner. Get them to write to you that way everything can be copied and filed then reply as a natural person asking for their proof of claim.

Proof of claim is proof of contract so no proof no contract means they get nothing; not one penny. More importantly they can't legally pursue you. I know they'll try to tell you to give them time to acquire this document, rubbish because it does not exist. No lawful contract exists between you and the debt collectors and none ever will. Understanding aspects of contract law is very important for survival at this game; if you don't know the rules of the game then how can you even participate. You will be eaten alive. These are the basic principles of contracting but there are also other forms of getting you into agreement with or without your written consent also without you even saying anything at all with "Persons" like the debt collectors or any other corporate entities, they use what's called "Tacit" agreements by getting you to contract by way of "Acquiescence".

To get a person into a Tacit Agreement with you is simple, especially if they are trying to extort money from you all you need to do is Conditionally Accept. Once again Conditional Acceptance removes any controversy because you are agreeing to pay, hence eliminating any court involvement so you're dealing with the matter by way of direct discussion. Now you have already agreed to pay any money they are claiming you owe in full, lawfully of course and only upon the condition that they provide you with the necessary paperwork which is their Proof Of Claim i.e. a Contract. They are now obligated to do so, this request should be sent by recorded delivery as your first letter and copies and receipts should be filed just in case these people are not too bright and decide they'll try to take this to court you have all the evidence you need to have it thrown out or to get judgement if need be.

In your Letter 1 you must allow them some time, be considerate. Allow them about 10 days to produce a lawful contract, also explaining your willingness to comply but with conditions always attached. It should also contain what recourse can be expected if they don't produce anything and/or if you suffered any damages in the process they will;

1. Be held culpable;
2. Agree to pay all fee schedules;
3. Pay three times what they are claiming you owe.

Oh how I love this bit because they now know it's not a matter of if, but when they fail to provide proof of claim, because in the end they'll probably be made to pay you instead for making false accusations and it also lets them know that now you mean business.

After 10 days have passed you'll probably not hear from them or if you do they would send you a response to inform you that they are trying their best to deal with your request and that you should be patient with them What? Not long ago they were demanding and threatening you to pay them or else, now it's please sir can you give us more time. Rubbish! This is where you write Letter 2, it's a bit more of letter 1 but reinforcing the facts laid out in your first letter and expressing your great disappointment, that this matter is still unresolved due to the fact that they are now inconveniencing you with their delays.

A further 10 days have passed and still no Proof Of Claim has been presented to you so that means if for some reason you have heard from them it is because their still begging for more time, stalling, but why? It's not as if the contract fairy is going to sprinkle some fairy dust on a piece of paper and magically produce one, I don't think so! Letter 3 is your next move; it's a notice, a Letter Of Default. You're now informing the bloodsuckers that their game is up, check mate, they're not allowed anymore time and you have had enough. It is in this letter you now state the following as facts:

1. They have no legal standing
2. They are a third party interloper
3. Their claim is fraudulent
4. That any damages you suffer, they will be held culpable.

Also this matter has now been resolved and closed so any further contact will now be unwarranted and will constitute as breach of our Tacit Agreement and will be meet by the penalty of a charge, usually in the sum of £1000 per infringement which seems like a nice round number to me.

Last but not least, after no contact has been made by your claimant of a 30 day period, it is time for your Letter 4 which is the "Estoppel". This is not a letter as such, it is more of a "Notice" sent by you addressed to your claimant to bind your tacit agreement by engraving it in legal stone. It is your Permanent and Irrevocable Estoppel by Acquiescence which will prevent any comebacks, forevermore barring them from bringing any and all claims, legal actions, orders, demands, lawsuits, costs, levies, penalties, damages, interests, liens and expenses whatsoever, against you or future contact of any kind or there will be serious legal repercussions of an epic scale.

As far as the law is concerned you have followed and adhered to it as any law knowing and abiding citizen would. To know your rights is the only way of being able to enforce them competently that it may give you great power, power you never thought you could possibly possess so you can defend any wrongful and unlawful action taken or perpetrated against you and your family successfully. The thing is, this is only the tip of the iceberg.

Black's Law Dictionary

Tacit: Silent; not expressed; implied or inferred; manifested by the refraining from contradiction or objection; inferred from the situation and circumstances, in the absence of express matter. Thus, tacit consent is consent inferred from the fact that the party kept silence when he had an opportunity to forbid or refuse.

Acquiescence: To give an implied consent to a transaction, to the accrual of a right, or to any act, by one's mere silence, or without express assent or acknowledgement.

Bouvier's Law Dictionary

Consideration (Contracts): A compensation which is paid, or all inconvenience suffered by the, party from whom it proceeds. Or it is the reason which moves the contracting party to enter into the contract. Viner defines it to be a cause or occasion meritorious, requiring a mutual recompense in deed or in law. Consideration of some sort or other, is so absolutely necessary to the forming a good contract, that a nudum pactum, or an agreement to do or to pay anything on one side, without any compensation to the other, is totally void in law, and a man cannot be compelled to perform it.

Estoppel (Pleading): a preclusion, in law, which prevents a man from alleging or denying a fact, in consequence of his own previous act, allegation or denial of a contrary tenor.

Chapter 5

Money

Is Money Real?

I think people are very confused and have their own opinions when it comes to understanding what the value of money is, or more likely does money have any real value at all? Some say money is not real, its worthless pieces of paper, while others say it has to be real because you can buy stuff with it, and then there are those that say it represents our real wealth held by the treasury. I think first we need to know what money really is. Simply put it's anything we can use to exchange for goods and services, yes that's it. That is the definition of money. It can be food, clothes, labour, shelter, a skill, gold, silver, rocks whatever we have that someone wants or needs even pieces of paper with numbers printed on them. Once someone is willing to exchange a thing for something else "Barter", that thing becomes money. The notes in our pocket are used as money but it is not money per se, it is what's called "Fiat" Currency or Central Bank Notes or Bills, understand, no?

Ok, so let's ask the question again, if you're talking about Fiat Currency, which is Central Bank Notes, is it real or have any real value? Well to answer this lets look to the Central Bank, the institution responsible for issuing these notes, let's see what they say on the matter. On their website they define Fiat Currency as notes printed by the central bank that is without intrinsic value which means it's not backed by gold or silver, declared by a government to be legal tender based solely on the faith of the people. Hang on a minute, based solely on the Faith of the People, is that it? No gold, no silver, no diamonds, nothing but faith? Most of the world's paper money is fiat money. Fiat money is not linked to any physical reserves like gold or silver so it risks becoming worthless due to hyperinflation. Also if people lose faith in a nation's paper currency, the money will no longer hold any value. So my faith is the only thing that gives it value, huh, great, need I say more?

So fiat money is of real value as long as the people say it is. If tomorrow we woke up and decided that we would stop using it cause we no longer had any faith in the current monetary system and say started writing amounts in terms of value on pieces of paper and use them as IOUs and in turn, someone was willing to put faith in it until I gave them something of value at a later time, then isn't that money? Yes normal pieces of paper with my handwriting on it, once accepted by someone for say food or a haircut or whatever service they require is money. Eureka! I cracked it, ok let me explain it in more simple terms.

One day I walked into my usual cafe for some breakfast as I do most mornings before work, I say hello to the chef and his staff then I ordered my usual as I take a seat so I can humour myself with the daily paper. I enjoy a bit of banter with the chef as I often do while having my breakfast and a strong cup of black coffee. Then after stuffing my face I thank them for another fantastic meal as I approach the counter to pay only to realise I had left my wallet at home, doh! You could just imagine the embarrassed look on my face but the chef knows me so I'm sure he'll trust me to pay at a later date, so I ask him if I could. He accepts that

Recreating Reality

I'll pay later and trusts me to do so but I kind of feel bad that I had to have him trust me so what I do is write on a piece of paper the amount for the food, plus a tip, of course then I sign it and date it and I tell the chef to hang on to this apparently worthless paper until I come back tomorrow and I'll exchange it for the type of money which he requires.

What I've done was created money out of thin air, out of trust just like the central bank does. Once the chef put his trust in my IOU it became valuable, legal tender, it became worth whatever amount was written on it to the same value of the bank notes that he required. Did I just perform magic? No, just practiced common sense. My piece of paper is of real value because if I decided that I wasn't going to pay him, he now had physical evidence that I owed him an amount and I could now be summoned before court if need be. I signed and dated a document with an amount I promised to pay to a person at a later date that was accepted, this is what's called a "Promissory Note" also known as a "Bill Of Exchange" So to get back to what your money is, oh I mean what bank notes are, it is nothing more than Promissory Notes no different than my piece of paper which I wrote on except for one thing, my note has no interest attached to it therefore creating no debt whatsoever. I could have also paid or exchanged it with the chef by providing a service instead of fiat money like fixing his coffee machine or washing dishes, couldn't I? Well, if that was what he wanted as payment.

There are loads of clues as to what you're using and calling it money, just look at what it's referred to for instance "Notes" and "Bills" but I guess the biggest giveaway that your bank notes are promissory notes and bills of exchange is the words written across it which reads " I Promise To Pay The Barer The Sum Of". Come on now that's just too blatant to ignore especially if your familiar with the Bills Of Exchange Act 1882, (a must read) but what does the barer get paid in the sum of? It's not gold or silver because we know that it's not backed by anything as the central bank told us on their official website, so what do we get if we decided to stroll down to the bank and wanted it exchanged for something of same value? Well I'll tell you the answer, it's nothing absolutely nothing, unless you want your note changed for another bank note or maybe you'll get some coins of same value of course.

There's more to these bank notes than meets the eye. We take for granted that the sum of money we earn when we are employed is all ours because we get paid for the work we carry out, right? Nothing could be further from the truth because we get paid in promissory notes, bills of exchange that were manufactured by the central bank, which was borrowed by the government in turn for use by us but with a condition attached, that condition is interest. Interest is the most important factor in this monetary equation. Every single note, bill and coin there is in existence today has interest attached to it that has to keep being repaid to the central bank. Every single penny created has been borrowed so let's just think about what that means for a minute. It does not belong to us, it's not ours so that means even my notes which I've earned, saved, broke my back and well literally slaved for carries debt attached to it that has to one day be repaid back to the central bank with the interest, so don't you ever forget that interest.

> "If money is the bond binding me to human life, binding society to me, binding me and nature and man, is not money the bond of all bonds? Can it not dissolve and bind all ties? Is it not, therefore, the universal agent of separation?"
> **Karl Marx – The Communist Manifesto**

> "Want of money and the distress of a thief can never be alleged as the cause of his thieving, for many honest people endure greater hardships with fortitude. We must therefore

seek the cause elsewhere than in want of money, for that is the miser's passion, not the thief's."

William Blake

"There is no intrinsic worth in money but what is alterable with the times, and whether a guinea goes for twenty pounds or for a shilling, it is the labour of the poor and not the high and low value that is set on gold or silver, which all the comforts of life must arise from."

Bernard Mandeville

"The price we have to pay for money is sometimes liberty."

Robert Louis Stevenson

Debt

There is one thing that scares people more than death itself and that is being in debt. It's stressful beyond measure. It makes people sick, act crazy and get angry with themselves just by the mere thought of being in it. No one wants to be in debt or remain in debt, but we all are and some of us don't even know it. Without even realising we are, the entire country we live in is getting deeper and deeper into debt not because of our lifestyles but because of the way the system has been designed. If this does not change now, it is only going to go in one direction and inevitably, that is down and in flames.

We have put the control of our countries money which is used by all of us into the hands of private financial institutions that print and create all of our currency which is then filtered into general circulation. Besides what the High Street Banks are secretly doing, how it works is money is loaned to the government at a specified rate of interest that has to be then paid back at some point in the near future. There is a major flaw with this system and the problem is the interest, so what does that actually mean to us? I understand some people have a fair bit of money in the bank so they may be deemed ok, aren't they? We live in a society where the more money you earn the better off you would seem to be and that's easy to see but unless you understand that all the money you now possess will one day be recuperated and repossessed by the institutions that issued it, for every note created has interest attached to it. It's either that or it will totally collapse and become worthless. Well if you don't believe that this is what's eventually going to happen then there's no need for you to worry, is there?

We can begin to see the tide changing already. The national debt continues to rise at an astonishing rate regardless of the many spending cuts and austerity measures the government has implemented. People getting kicked out of their houses because they cannot continue to afford their mortgage payments whether it's the rises in interest rates or it's pay cuts or you might have lost your job altogether due to cutbacks. We see deflation in our currency so now our saving and pensions are worth less than they were while inflation sky rockets and the cost of living seems nearly impossible to cope with. Some of our properties are now worth a lot less than what we paid for it and it is now in what we call negative equity and at the same time renting is getting more expensive so either way our wages are stretched to the limit at every avenue. Utility bills have all gone up and keep going up so we're always having to make cutbacks in our general spending on food, clothing, travel, education, holidays, childcare, entertainment, even all our little luxuries have now gone and the children's activities have been restricted to a minimum. What is going on is the global collection of due loan repayments and charges attributed to all the central bank issued notes. These financial systems we're bound to are the products of the people's perceived reality brought on from our own lack of involvement and understanding about the inner working mechanisms of money creation.

The clues are right in front our faces but we are still oblivious to the fact of what's really being perpetrated by hidden forces, controlling our leaders like string puppets. All the money that was ever created by this system has to be returned to the lenders, the private banks and also the Bank of England. It is a private Central Bank, yes, private! Some dispute this fact but you can go to their website to read their ambiguous statements and judge for yourself. We the people have to pay them back with interest. It doesn't make sense I know, it is impossible to comprehend for the simple fact, let's say for example, somehow we were able to acquire every single bank note and coin in existence, then pay it back to the private banking institutions that lent us all this money, we should be ok and there would be no more debt, right? Wrong, because you will still have to pay the interest on almost two trillion pounds, or did you forget? So tell me, where are we going to get this extra money from? All the money ever created, printed or coined has been repaid so we don't have any more notes to pay the interest with, but wait we can borrow some more money again, to pay back what we still owe in interest, wait a minute here, that doesn't make sense, that's just dumb. But that's exactly what we're doing at the moment.

You see the system isn't broken, so there is no point trying to fix it. That would be impossible as this is the way it was made, by design, to be what it is today, an elaborate plan to enslave us all with debt. We must now discard this old system for it is a vicious creature that has tricked us to believe it was our servant, when in fact it was created to place every man, woman and child into financial bondage. We must now create a new system, a system of balance and equality, one that would benefit mankind and work together in harmony, with great excellence so perfectly and sustainable that it would make the other obsolete, it is the only option left. We have been on the receiving end of one of the greatest hoaxes in history, made to believe in the retarded system in use today which makes no sense whatsoever. It is incredibly unsustainable and is consuming us slowly, so why are we still using this corrupt system? The truth is, I really don't know. Maybe we're too stupid or too busy or distracted or just don't care to understand the inner workings of the financial establishment that we depend on, but if I somehow wanted to have complete control over everything and everyone in this world, this corrupt system is the system I would use.

"No pecuniary consideration is more urgent, than the regular redemption and discharge of the public debt: on none can delay be more injurious, or an economy of time more valuable."
George Washington, 1973

"Debt is an ingenious substitute for the chain and whip of the slave driver."
Ambrose Bierce

"I had a wholesome dread of the consequences of running in debt."
Frederick Douglass

Banks

"A License to Print Money" we've heard this expression many times before. Well secretly this is what our banking institutions have in their possession, yes literally. As you already know from the chapter on money, Fiat currency is the chosen method of use by our governments because of the simple fact that we are broke. Yes people, broke! Oh I'm sorry I meant Bankrupt, as it is the more acceptable terminology used, why do you think we borrow money from the Private Central Bank in the first place? Do you think it's because this country's got a great line of credit and it looks good on our fictitious credit ratings? I don't think so.

You would think banks work solely for our benefit, after all they're securing our hard earned cash from the criminals which are apparently lurking in the dark, waiting for the right moment to relieve us of all our savings, wouldn't you? But who would think that the greedy bankers were the ones we needed to be weary of. Banks now control all of our financial activity, whether were employed or not we need an account with them so we can access funds or make transactions, receive payments, get loans, credit cards, pay bills, buy food and get mortgages whatever it may be. They control the flow of money and that's some damn good control to have.

In the early days we used to entrust the bank with our precious metals (gold and silver) and we would trade the notes we received for our deposits instead, these were issued by the bank for the commodities we needed with the option for us to return those notes to the bank in exchange for our gold, hence the wording on these notes to this day which reads "I Promise To Pay The Barer On Demand The Sum Of" which was whatever the value written on that note to the equal value in gold or silver can be reclaimed. It is from silver where the term "Sterling" for the pound in England derived, obviously it would denote the weight in sterling silver to the equal value of that note.

So now the true wealth, the real and physical value of money is a thing of the past and we now use the valueless Fiat Currency, this is why the bankers are rubbing their grubby little hands together with a big grin from ear to ear. You see bank notes, actual cash which is in your pocket counts for less than 10% of all the money in the world, the other 90% is what's referred to as Digital Currency. This is just one of ways the banks use their licence, to get away with fraud, yes you heard me right, fraud on an epic scale. When you deposit your funds into a bank it's no longer your property, it's now the Bank's money, you just handed it over willingly. You may be shocked but they now own it legally, its theirs and they'll use your funds as they see fit by making investments, loans, trading on the stock market or just for money creation by what is known in the industry as "Fractional Reserve Banking."

Lending money in the conventional sense is where I have £20 and I loan you that £20, I could even require you pay a bit of interest although interest was deemed immoral and illegal in the early days but this practice is very straight forward, right, makes sense but what banks do is participate in "Money Creation" or "Fractional Reserve Banking" where money is loaned out of up to nine times to what they have in their reserves, but how is this possible and is it even ethical? The banks literally print money through the use of Digital Currency, they don't have to actually have the paper notes in their reserves to loan out and they never do, but by just typing on a few computer keys and hey presto, your account has now been credited. So if I was a bank and I had £20, that's all, I could now loan you £180, but get this I can and will also charge interest on this money even though I never had it in the first place, so in the end, for the banks it's a win-win situation. Even if panic broke out and there was a "Run" on the banks where all their depositors wanted their cash out for some reason, obviously there won't be enough money in their reserves to return everyone's deposits because of their financial fraudulent practice which they have been abusing way beyond their means. This will ultimately cause them to go bankrupt. But don't fear the government will then step in and bail them out with your tax contributions despite their reckless behaviour because banking institutions are seen as too integral to the economy or maybe it's because they are far too influential and powerful to be allowed to fail.

The problem with this system is the banks work as a money vacuum that sucks the economy dry of all the money in circulation and when that becomes limited they then come for your property when you can't keep up with the payments. When this happens it has to be replenished by the government using what they call "Quantitive Easing" which is really just borrowing more money so they can then filter some of it back into the economy which funny enough will create more debt and more instability later on, crazy huh? No wonder the world's financial situation is in such a mess but instead of creating a new system that can be self sustaining, they keep throwing more fuel onto the fire, the fire that has already been burning out of control for some considerable time now, and hope somehow it may extinguish itself at some point. The book *The Creature From Jekyll Island* written by G. Edward Griffin reveals how the American Central Bank, the Federal Reserve was created and how it deceives the taxpayer and influences the flow of money.

How much higher can they keep raising the debt ceiling? Are we still at the edge of that fiscal cliff or are we now falling to our doom? Such terminology is being used to explain the absolute limit to our borrowing and it's all made up, fictional just like their bank notes and debt but that doesn't stop the deficit. It just keeps growing bigger by the day and no one in charge thinks that maybe this system just isn't working anymore. The math just isn't adding up but hey, someone's got to be making all that money, right? I mean all the money just doesn't disappear into thin air. It's obviously going somewhere, in someone's very deep pockets, right? It's just not that guy who's killing himself, holding down two jobs and misses quality time with his family so he can pay his mortgage and feed his kids, come on! Something is seriously wrong with this picture. Someone knows, our leaders are not that stupid although I'd like to think they are from the lousy results they produce. So what they're doing must be for some specific purpose, why is this system still in place, maybe it's a conspiracy, who knows? But whatever it may be we are the ones government refer to as the people and society, everything they do should be in our interest but for whatever reason, we don't seem to be part of that plan.

> "I believe that banking institutions are more dangerous to our liberties than standing armies. If the American people ever allow private banks to control the issue of their currency, first by inflation, then by deflation, the banks and corporations that will grow up around [the banks] will deprive the people of all property until their children wake-up homeless on the continent their fathers conquered. The issuing power should be taken from the banks and restored to the people, to whom it properly belongs."
>
> **Thomas Jefferson, 1802**

"It is well enough that people of the nation do not understand our banking and monetary system, for if they did, I believe there would be a revolution before tomorrow morning."
Henry Ford

"The rich run a global system that allows them to accumulate capital and pay the lowest possible price for labour. The freedom that results applies only to them. The many simply have to work harder, in conditions that grow ever more insecure, to enrich the few. Democratic politics, which purports to enrich the many, is actually in the pocket of those bankers, media barons and other moguls who run and own everything."
Charles Moore

Alternative Money

Now that we know what money really is we can start to engage with each other using an alternative, free from the stronghold of the bank notes and their hyper inflated interest and charges that are enslaving us in debt. We can turn back the clock and begin using barter once again as one way of trading goods for services and vice versa. We just need to start putting our trust back into the people instead of the private bank notes. This will not be easy I know but nevertheless it has become necessary.

The use of precious metals like gold and silver is one idea a lot of people would like to revert to but there are a few drawbacks to consider if we were to engage in this type of monetary system. Firstly there is the problem of availability; the only ways to possess these metals are to purchase them, which would defeat the purpose in the first place, or to acquire by mining, well that is not an option we have. Then we have to consider the value, the price as we know is determined by the private central bank via the monetary policy decisions made by them related to the interest rates so basically it's only worth what they say it's worth, or what someone is willing to pay for it. Even making small purchases will be hampered by trying to give the right amount of gold to the price of the commodity. There is also the issue of its supply and demand however unlike most other commodities at the moment, saving and disposal plays a larger role in affecting its price than its consumption.

Hoarding precious metals might seem like a good idea in preparation for the inevitably approaching total collapse of our financial system but there are other issues we need to take into consideration, like maybe our security could be a problem. After all where is the safest place for us to store our last remaining wealth when bank notes are no more? Under our mattresses? Certainly not any of the banks, if any survived, yea right! We now run the risk of losing it all, either by getting mugged by the desperate people who will just be trying to survive or robbed by the same institutions we entrusted with our money that brought about total currency failure. Confiscation of gold was perpetrated before in the U.S. upon the people of the land in 1933, Executive Order 6102 and it can and probably will be done again, and history has a funny way of repeating itself.

Another option is Digital currency. There are various types of digital currency. One is electronic money that acts as an alternative currency. Currently, alternative digital currencies are not produced by government-endorsed central banks nor are they necessarily backed by national currency which for us is a good thing. It differs from virtual money used in virtual economies due to its use in transactions with real goods and services so it is not only limited to circulation within online games. Digital currencies are often backed by a promise to pay a set amount of gold or silver bullion in exchange for each of its units while others float against whatever individuals are willing to exchange for it. The nature of digital currency mirrors that of paper money as a means of payment. It is similar to sending a £10 note in the mail and as such, digital currency; Electronic Payment Systems follow this same process. Like all forms of money there is also the risk of losing all of your online investments for the simple fact that it is only data and no more than that. As we know data can be corrupted, intercepted, hacked, stolen or systems can crash altogether. You see the point I'm trying to make is that no form of money whether paper, valuable metals or digital is totally 100% guaranteed to financially sustain you in the future without some chance of losing every single penny.

The question you have to ask yourself is, what is the purpose of accumulating some of your wealth if the worst was to happen? I'm sure the number one thing on the top of everyone's list would be the exact same thing, it's something that we definitely need the most and when the manure is about to hit the fan it is most important to our survival, yes you guessed it food. Sustenance, food and water, this is what in the end will be more important to everyone not money, gold, silver or diamonds so unless your digestive system can break down these elements I suggest you acquire some land and start growing some crops. The more self sufficient we can be; the less dependent on the monetary system we will be. This independence will empower us, great strength will bring about our total freedom, and then our future will be guaranteed.

At the moment we treat our most precious resource with great disdain and take for granted that it can never run out or if too much of it becomes contaminated we can always use our filtration systems to make it suitable for human consumption. We are not taking into consideration where all of our food comes from and what the plants need in its soil to nourish it that it may produce what we eat. When water is available no more and what remains has too many toxins we'll have a grave problem. We will be facing extinction. It's all well and good to take care of your business and do what you need to do to secure your future here and now but that's all it may be, your future. What about the generations after you? So besides through investment in agriculture as we now know is the most valuable and only true form of money, we also need to take a stand, make a form of personal protest by boycotting and participating in divestment of any and all companies or corporations that bring about harm to our world, our only home. And when they abuse, destroy, pollute, contaminate, congest, kill, steal, act unlawful or violate any of our inalienable rights it then becomes our duty to act, to fight back, we now become obligated to do so.

> "You gotta make a change. It's time for us as a people to start making some changes, let's change the way we eat, let's change the way we live, and lets change the way we treat each other. You see the old way wasn't working so it's on us, to do what we gotta do to survive."
>
> **Tupac Shakur**

> "Wealth consists not in having great possessions, but in having few wants."
>
> **Epictetus**

Chapter 6

Corporations

Greed Is Good?

As a child growing up you were always told how to behave, the do's and don'ts; the rights and wrongs; what's expected of you in this life. You were taught the importance of sharing with your siblings, your friends, even strangers and especially the less fortunate. Where has that culture of generosity, kindness and love gone? Now we are adults, working for some major corporation and the motto has become 'Greed Is Good'. Why have we now become the perpetrators of what we were told to never let ourselves be? Maybe the reason is that we're being rewarded for it and very well in fact for some of us anyway, for being greedy, ruthless and conniving. Take a good, hard look at society; this is the world we accept to live in today. 'Greed Is Good' this is the motto of international corporations. The very foundation of their empire is to carry out whatever needs to be done, by any means necessary with the sole purpose of making profits.

The world that we live in is no longer seen through their eyes as a planet that sustains life to billions of people for prosperity, it has become no more than an object, an open market to exploit, a commodity to be bought and sold, property to be owned and controlled, with vast amounts of natural resources that are up for grabs by the ones who have the money, the influence and power, ones that crave more power, absolute power that they may acquire the status that not of kings but to be worshiped as gods. This is not the rational thinking you would expect of a human being, one that aspires for the advancement and survival of all life on earth. It is without a doubt this bares the hallmarks and mentality of psychopaths. This is the essence of capitalism and this is what's trumpeted into your cranium as the best thing since sliced bread, the only way to progress but this couldn't be further from the truth; capitalism has failed us, enslaved us and destroying the planet in the process. We have been tricked to believe capitalism was in our interest, a chance for everyone to make it rich so we became blinded in pursuit of wealth, the idea was pure fantasy, as we can now see it was only meant for a elite few who has cornered the marketplace and with the looming fact of an inevitable economic collapse, an alternative is greatly required to replace a failing system but yet again we seem ever reluctant to replace it. It's funny the idea of implementing a socialist economy have been demonised for so many years by our governments but it has been flourishing in so-called communist China which constantly shows around 8%, one of the highest growth of Gross Domestic Product (GDP) in the world.

Greed has overcome common sense and is so sad but true to see what we have become, a machine, a mindless zombie serving the masters, following every instruction which we execute without empathy for they promise us the world for the mere cost of the price of our soul. I quite understand the predicament people are in. It is a form of entrapment. We were made to believe that competition is good, it is healthy, it's what makes us strong, and it's for our own good, but what about the losers? Let's bare a thought for all the losers. For there to be a winner someone has got to lose the game and the losers are far too often the ones who are the majority of people. The losers are always the unemployed, the homeless, the sick, the elderly, the single mums, minimum wage workers, middle income families, public servants, carers, the self employed, the tradesmen and women, teachers, nurses, the farmers, the butchers and even the military and police. Funny enough most of the same people sacrificing and busting their rump for the corporate bloodsuckers agenda end up getting shafted as well, adding to the problem. Most of these people are trapped with few or no options left, they need to pay the bills and feed their families so they take the only jobs that are available to them even if it means doing something that they're morally against.

These corporations control every aspect our daily lives in order to keep you in a state of dependency whether that's through fear, hate, greed or insecurity in order to obtain their goals of keeping you consuming, that they may continue making obscene amounts of loot. We consume at an alarming rate whatever is manufactured by the corporate public relations executives, the propaganda engineers that bombard every one of our senses, our feeling and emotions with the use of the mainstream media which they also dominate so we will never stop shopping. Misinformation is a great adversary to combat, but to see through the wall of deception is by far not an easy task; the odds are highly stacked against us, it is everything, it is everywhere, and it is everyone.

This fight is an easy one to lose because you are up against yourself, your ego. Remember the ego is not your true self. Only the true you can bring about the change you want to see in your life, your reality. To ask others to join in your battle would be unfair to them because they might not see as you see; they might not be ready mentally to decipher the matrix of the accepted paradigm although by your actions their curiosity may be fuelled. They might become inspired and start to question the ideology set before them. This is your choice to make a difference and believe me one person can. The easier fight is with these corporations that harm the environment and run their business like slave labour camps which care only about one thing, money. We direct our cash elsewhere depriving them of it and they lose their power it's that simple. One by one as we start to wake up and realize our own strength we will come to understand that we are the ones in charge and they are dependent on our compliance, our participation and our investment in their hyper inflated and non essential commodities. The sooner we begin to take back control the sooner they will return to their rightful place being subservient to the human race and the earth, treating it again like our home.

"Power corrupts and absolute power corrupts absolutely"
George Orwell - 1984

"The greatest victory in life is to rise above the material things that we once valued most."
Muhammad Ali

"We don't have to engage in grand, heroic actions to participate in the process of change. Small acts, when multiplied by millions of people, can transform the world."
Howard Zinn

"Earth provides enough to satisfy every man's needs, but not every man's greed."
Mahatma Gandhi

"Their final objective toward which all their deceit is directed is to capture political power so that, using the power of the state and the power of the market simultaneously, they may keep the common man in eternal subjection."
Henry A. Wallace - Democracy Reborn

Control

We live our lives with the belief that we are free, free to make whatever choices we so desire so long as that which we desire is within the laws set by our government or by what is considered acceptable in the eyes of society. But what if even those choices were influenced and limited somehow so no matter what we decided, in the end the result wasn't what we really thought we wanted in the first place. The choices that are presented before us would be like asking someone if they would rather have the steak or the chicken when in fact they are vegetarian. It's like this in most of the options we presume to have. Take politics as one example, you have the left wing politicians and the right wing politicians but what they don't tell you is that both wings are two parts of the same big, ugly bird.

We have been duped into believing that democracy exists, that we have real choice, a say in who we want to run the country and represent us and all we have to do is pick one, just use your vote after you have considered all the candidates and their policies, right? But how can we make an informed decision on who is most suitable to lead us when our choices have been limited to the two or three major parties? We now have a system where both major parties have the financial backing of the same mega corporations, funding their campaigns and contributing enormous donations, influencing the policies being made that affect our daily lives, obviously so it may be in their favour for tax breaks or defence contracts or construction or infrastructure, shall

I go on? What chances, if any have we got? Most people never hear of any other parties or their mandates, it's like they don't even exist. And if you do happen to hear about them making some headway soon enough they'll be slandered and mocked by smear campaigns being run by the major opponents, making them appear to be crazy, extremist or unpatriotic so you will immediately dismiss them straight away without any second thought.

These days there is no difference between Labour, Conservative, or Liberal Democrat that's because they all work for the same master and that's not you. Sorry to burst your bubble but it's time for you to wake up; that is if you didn't already know. But some people do know the diabolic games being played at their expense and still they participate in this elaborate farce of see-saw voting every term like that dumbstruck teenager from the movie Twilight who couldn't make up her mind whether to be with the vampire or the werewolf, either way she was choosing a monster. These monsters agree on most issues while trying to scare everyone into believing it's all the fault of the immigrants stealing their jobs or the poor on benefits that are too lazy to work, putting a strain on the economy or maybe it's your fault for not handling your finances properly and living on too much credit. The truth is that once our government has been lobbied by large corporations, that is where their interest will lie, so there will always be corruption and the people will always have to bear the burden. Why do you think there is so much corporate funding towards political campaigns? It is so they make certain the ones they want you to vote for are seen the most and seen in the very best image as though there was no other possible choice to be made but the ones they choose for you and definitely not by you.

Advertising has become a tool of the corporate conman not for you to make an educated decision on an availability of a commodity in line with your needs but to imply that theirs is most superior with no other option possibly conceivable in order for you to make yourself a better person. I must say though, we are very gullible and easily swayed. We lap up everything, every moving picture and sound that comes out of that little box in our living rooms called the television, no wonder what we watch on it is appropriately called televised programming. Since we were children it was our environment, our babysitter and teacher, influencing our young minds on their obscure version of reality. The television moulded our brain and how we think and process information over time without us consciously knowing; influencing our every emotions, judgment, behaviour and attitudes by using clever tricks like subliminal messages or subliminal perception and suggestive themes to get us to become drones, making us act like zombies, walking around dragging our feet, with an endless urge to continually consume, unaware of the real world unfolding around us. Majority of people form their general views, opinions, personalities, beliefs and attitudes from their environment and society. When that society then limits the spectrum of information and debate you get a population of people that lack the ability to deviate from the rhetoric of conformity due to their limited knowledge, leading to an inability of critical thinking.

Our children are our future and if you are too busy to protect and guide them from having their intuitive minds destroyed, therefore being controlled by the influences of what we deem to call entertainment today, it's your own fault. This version of entertainment we subject our kids to in the form of cartoons, mini-series, movies, so called reality TV and now also interactive computer games are getting increasingly worrying with the type of content they tend to portray, attracting their curiosity in a negative direction. The video games especially, for one they are getting more and more violent and realistic, rewarding the players for the most kills and promoting you as a hero for it. They're often designed around military style combats as though it is the intention to glamorise war, to normalise it and desensitise the players of the true reality, the casualties, mental trauma, the repercussions and the very real dangers of what it's actually like to engage in military invasion. What messages are we sending to our young minds when we expose them to this warped version of warfare, how well they can execute their orders, killing is fun or are they training our children as soldiers to eventually go to war? The US Constitution, inspired by The Magna Carta enshrined the rights and freedoms of the people which they already have and will always have, to be able to invoke and enforce them at will but this is ever and increasingly under attack by the same powers with their false promises. If we were to relinquish some or all of those rights, giving complete control over to the government or whoever is really calling all the shots, then we will be made safer from threats to our existence both foreign and domestic. I think not!

> "I see in the near future a crisis approaching that unnerves me and causes me to tremble for the safety of my country.... corporations have been enthroned and an era of corruption in high places will follow, and the money power of the country will endeavour to prolong its reign by working upon the prejudices of the people until all wealth is aggregated in a few hands and the Republic is destroyed."
>
> **Abraham Lincoln**

> "They who can give up essential liberty to obtain a little temporary safety deserve neither liberty nor safety"
>
> **Benjamin Franklin**

> "Forget the politicians. The politicians are put there to give you the idea you have freedom of choice. You don't. You have no choice. You have owners. They own you. They own everything."

"They don't want a population of citizens capable of critical thinking. They don't want well informed, well educated people capable of critical thinking. They're not interested in that. That doesn't help them."

George Carlin – Life Is Worth Losing

CHAPTER 7

The Government

Does Government Work?

Now that's a good question. It will achieve different answers depending on who you ask. It could be a personal thing or it could be coming from a different perspective like looking at the bigger picture, for instance incorporating everyone in society. But by looking at the way things are at present you might draw the conclusion that they are not operating in the best interest of the people, the very same people who put them into office to represent them, but instead they cater for some other external entity which always seems to have a hell of a lot of hard cash to their disposal and always seem to get all the tax breaks, incentives, government contracts, subsidies, funding, statutes, bills and acts of parliament passed in their favour to make an obscene amount of money, just to point out. So with this in mind, I don't know what your position might be when it comes to whether or not you believe the government is a competent functional organisation that operates for the purpose it was formed but I'm sure you could make an assumption as to where I stand on this subject.

Democracy, I often wonder if the thing really exists, even if the very word has any relevance in today's society. I guess democracy is like magic, you know that it really doesn't exist but it gives you the illusion that it is real. Maybe it was at one point in the past when there were real choices to be made and real leaders to choose from that actually cared about the welfare, freedom and justice of its people but all we're left with is parasites, manipulating and manufacturing the illusions of choice. You think you have choice? Well of course you do, you can chose from the options they provide for you, that's all. It's like offering twenty-five different types of tea to a coffee drinker, I'm not going to accept tea just because you don't serve coffee, I'll have to go find somewhere that does, or I'll grind my own. And that's the real reason why, my friends, I never vote. I'm still looking for somewhere serving coffee. We no longer have an effective government that serves the people, instead we have the very same public servants force feeding us garbage constantly and telling us it's yummy apple pie and that all they do is for the greater good, but you never see them eating any of it. Politicians have made us believe that somehow we are subordinate to them, that we are the servants and they are our masters, there is a reason the title bestowed upon them is public servants you know.

In all the years that I've know government, as far as I can remember, I've never really seen it as being an effective instrument for bringing about peace, freedom, sustainability and balance. There is also the ever widening gap between the very few wealthy individuals and the vast amount of the poor population in their country. Aren't these the very simple things we, the majority of people desire to be solved, so why aren't they listening to us? Why are we being ignored by the same people we put into office to represent us? They spend the country's budget indiscriminately on programmes of little or no significant importance, while cutting spending on health, welfare, homelessness, education and disease research to name a few but war, oh I'm sorry

I mean defence, there's always money for that even though no one is invading us. It is clear to see they're not interested in using money to eradicate poverty their interest is eradicating people to make money. We want peace, to be able to wake up in the morning without hearing about some new invasion being planned, bombs being dropped by drones killing innocent civilians, war on terror, war on drugs, and war on whistleblowers, what's next? War on our human rights, war on free speech, war on protesters, war on civil liberties? This is coming soon believe me and it sounds like a dictatorship to me. We can never be truly free if we consider someone our enemy. Without global peace how can we ever have security? Our government wants wars, it's a necessity you must understand, they try to convince us but its only beneficial for those which are involved within those invested parties, financially dependent on war if not we would instead have wars on disease, wars on greed, wars on homelessness, wars on poverty, wars on unemployment, wars on ignorance, wars on corruption, wars on pollution, wars on hunger, wars on injustice. But we don't, why? There's no profit in it. We need to fight the real wars which are needed to be fought not the ones with arms and military but the ones that are plaguing our society every day. I hope you can see where I'm coming from.

It's inevitable, the horrific results we get from the appointed leaders, but what else did you expect? When did the wealthy, power craving, continuously lie telling, warmongering, scumbags ever put your wellbeing before theirs? They are not ordinary people that face the daily struggle like most of us, so how can they know what we're going through or even represent us? What, did you actually believe they would keep their election promises? Then you're more naive than a two year old and you have no one to blame but yourself for believing the trash that constantly falls out their mouth. But don't be too hard on yourself though, they're very good at convincing the unsuspecting public of all their trickery to get what they want and once they get it let me tell you, you could petition, poll, write letters and protest until you're blue in the face but you'll just get brushed off like a biscuit crumb that's fallen on their Armani sleeves. Until you have money, and lots of it, to compete with the Oligarchs and corporate elites that lobby or let's call it what it really is, bribe or buy those greedy, corrupt bastards, you're either invisible to these people or just a nuisance. In the end any protest you engage in will be dealt with by the police who are ever too eager to crack a few skulls. Let's be honest with ourselves, ministers of parliament are all very well off financially, also coming from wealthy families some worth millions, do you really think they know or care about the struggle of the ordinary person, the middle and low income earners, trying to get by in society? They are so disconnected from what our reality consist of it would be amazing if they could even try to imagine what it was like to walk a day in our shoes far more to represent us, it's ludicrous.

In any rational thinking society, or let's face it anywhere for that matter, where someone has been employed to competently carry out some function or service and failed miserably in every aspect of their field would be kicked to the curb, sacked immediately without question. So why in the world do we have to endure the pain and suffering of incompetent and corrupt leaders that we've lost all confidence in and also must wait an entire term before we can have some hope of change in order to vote in another puppet? It seems to me that there is no logic to this madness whatsoever, that we should blindly accept a system of this kind that restricts the people's voice all for the sake of clutching onto power. We are quite lucky there are some restrictions in government still, maintained by the few members of parliament with a conscience and enough balls to object to the ridiculous requests for unjust and illegal wars and laws the government continually tries to involve and impose on their people and country, but that too is ever diminishing. So to answer the question, does government work? Well in this capitalist society, if you belong the one percent bracket at the top of the pyramid of success, well I guess it's working perfectly.

> "Civil disobedience is not our problem. Our problem is civil obedience. Our problem is that people all over the world have obeyed the dictates of leaders…and millions have been killed because of this obedience…Our problem is that people are obedient all over the world in the face of poverty and starvation and stupidity, and war, and cruelty. Our problem is that people are obedient while the jails are full of petty thieves… (and) the grand thieves are running the country. That's our problem."
> **Howard Zinn, 1970**

> "Obviously I don't vote as I believe democracy is a pointless spectacle where we choose between two indistinguishable political parties, neither of whom represent the people but the interest of powerful business elites that run the world."
> **Russell Brand**

> "In the US, there is basically one party - the business party. It has two factions, called Democrats and Republicans, which are somewhat different but carry out variations on the same policies. By and large, I am opposed to these policies. As is most of the population."
> **Noam Chomsky, 2010**

> "Sometimes I wonder whether the world is being run by smart people who are putting us on or by imbeciles who really mean it."
> **Laurence J. Peter – The Peter Principle**

"Governments, if they endure, always tend increasingly toward aristocratic forms. No government in history has been known to evade this pattern. And as the aristocracy develops, government tends more and more to act exclusively in the interests of the ruling class -- whether that class be hereditary royalty, oligarchs of financial empires, or entrenched bureaucracy."

Frank Herbert – Children of Dune

"The oppressed are allowed once every few years to decide which particular representatives of the oppressing class are to represent and repress them."

Karl Marx

Politics

This form of political rhetoric practiced by governments upon the masses is commonly accepted as the norm, but why? It is a diabolical form of psychology and language, used against the public to confuse, trick, sway, distort, and downright lie about important information and promote their agendas, making the unacceptable seem acceptable. The word Politics derived from the Greek word **politikos**, meaning "*of, for, or relating to citizens*" it is the practice and theory of influencing other people on a civic or individual level. Some people might say it refers to achieving and exercising positions of governance by organized control over a society as a whole, particularly a state. In my opinion, I find it very worrying that it is widely accepted in most countries where a group of individuals can coerce and impose their ideology over an ill-informed population by inveigling them with baseless debates and making promises of change on a repetitive, endless cycle which are never kept.

Money and politics today seems to form a perfect relationship, they say the two goes hand in hand, but nothing could be further from the truth, money has no place in the political arena even though you have been made to accept this as a normal practice. If you're a large corporation or an independent with loads of cash you do what is called lobbying your member of parliament, where you can make a substantial "donation" to the party in order to influence decisions being made by government, basically bribes. This is absurd and should be illegal and immoral cause if it is not, then this means that the policy makers of your country are not the guys you voted for, it's the ones sitting in board rooms, smoking cigars, grabbing up the country's resources, paying little or no taxes, genetically modifying crops, injecting harmful chemicals in foods, destroying our environment, suppressing clean technology and the list goes on and on. People that don't understand politics vote; people that do understand politics start a revolution.

Let's face it, politics has been accepted as a very negative word for some time now because of all of the corruption and hypocrisy involved with government officials. Most people are also not fond of losing their freedoms and liberties more and more each day, statute laws of all manners being imposed upon them while their privacy and human rights continue to be violated constantly. Government always seem to manufacture some apparent reason for granting themselves more power than necessary and non of the responsibility or accountability, with their favourite excuse being "for the purpose of national security. "For some reason we are always facing possible attack, allegedly from some radical organisation and with the help of the mainstream media most people believe that their lives are in constant danger so they're willing to give up some of their liberties to facilitate the will of the state by having their rights trampled on and privacy invaded. The narrative perpetuated worldwide by government officials and media is that they are there to protect us from terrorists; that we're constantly under attack by foreign entities; well this is just not true if you care to look at statistics, see you are about 7 times more likely to be killed by a police officer than a terrorist, funny huh? I know which one I'm more concerned about as I have been stopped and harassed many times in the past by the police for no apparent reason, some of them with their bad attitude and their overzealous abuse of authority who are usually always armed, but I never once had any interactions, been threatened or felt like my life was in danger from someone you might refer to as an extremist, have you?

Political policies are responsible for the lack of information the general public are privy to, it is as though we are incapable of making an informed and intelligent decision on matters concerning our own welfare but if that was true, then why are we allowed to vote? Maybe we are as indecisive and incompetent as they think and keeping secrets from us are a necessity? I tend to differ. I believe we do know what's best for us, if we're treated like the rational thinking adults we are and if given the opportunity to be consulted with the truth over important matters of national security. Secrets, in my view are only needed when someone is trying to hide the truth, nothing else that's why I find the use of this policy by government to be morally repugnant behaviour. I guess if they gave the public full access to the ins and outs of what's really going on behind closed doors in the political arena we might have them all arrested and tried for treason, so all the secret keeping they participate in and say are to protect us is in fact really just to protect them from us and it's all a charade, an act, just theatre with pre-written scripts to keep us docile. So in the end you're left with a choice, you can make your voice heard by taking some form of a stand to bring about change or get a comfy chair, put your feet up and enjoy the show.

> "The very word "secrecy" is repugnant in a free and open society; and we are as a people inherently and historically opposed to secret societies, to secret oaths and to secret proceedings. We decided long ago that the dangers of excessive and unwarranted concealment of pertinent facts far outweighed the dangers which are cited to justify it."
> **John F. Kennedy, 1961**

> "The dangers of excessive and unwarranted concealment of pertinent facts, far outweigh the dangers that are cited to justify them. There is a very grave danger than an announced need for an increased need for security, will be seized upon

by those anxious to expand its meaning to the very limits of censorship and concealment. That I do not tend to permit, so long as it's in my control"

John F. Kennedy, 1961

"When the people fear the government there is tyranny, when the government fears the people there is liberty."

Thomas Jefferson

"Political language is designed to make lies sound truthful and murder respectable, and to give an appearance of solidity to pure wind."

George Orwell- Politics & the English Language

CHAPTER 8

The News

Corporate Media

Nearly all of the information we receive on a daily basis comes from the mainstream media, which means whatever which is reported is the only version and limits your knowledge on the subject unless you seek an alternative source. So you would think that the responsible and professional thing to do by these mega news corporations would be to just report the truth regardless of their opinion on the matter. I know what you're saying, but don't they report with an unbiased view about important information, and why would they lie to us anyway, right? The real question you should be asking is, have they lied to us before? Well to think of it, the answer is a resounding yes they have. There have been many times before where they had to face much criticism and publicly apologise for their breach of trust, sometimes even face legal action so with this in mind I guess we're now left asking, why?

You don't have to be an avid follower of the news to have caught out reporters making stuff up, participating in disinformation, blatantly lying, restricting information, having irrelevant debates, fabricating evidence or leaning towards a specific agenda, I know this for a fact. For me personally it's quite easy these days to recognise the scripted reporting amongst the multiple outlets and the limited spectrum of debate that is being portrayed as investigative journalism, it's a real joke to watch. Once the sacred vows of journalism have been broken by the media I no longer hold them as a reliable source for information, how can I? The trust I've put in the so called reputable, professionalism of the accredited journalist have been abused and betrayed on too many an occasion like an unfaithful partner you've once forgiven of infidelity has cheated and lied to you once again. It is clear to see now that the interests of the mainstream media are not one those of the public but of the ones who pay their wages and belong to their elite power circle of political and corporate influences. I now understand why rock artists used to always throw televisions out of their hotel windows.

Today we have a multitude of news stations, press, magazines and internet, bombarding us with their daily dose of programming. We're being indoctrinated by the media's ideology, repetitively being portrayed with the intention of influencing our psyche. This presumption of society's behaviour is in fact to coerce the collective consciousness of the people; this is accumulation of many major news corporations which are owned by just a few elite fat cats building an empire to rule over an ignorant and misguided population. It's not difficult to be influenced by whatever we continuously read in the press or see on television so it's no surprise how easily we may be swayed towards any agenda of the so called ruling class or political interest, which usually results in them ultimately gaining more power, getting richer and us losing more freedoms, increased consumption, having to pay more for everything, getting less, enduring pay cuts as a result and being easily manipulated and controlled by living in fear. But there's hope, they aren't all out to brainwash you into total submission, there are actually honest, hard working, real journalists out there doing their best to bring you the truth, you just have to open your eyes a bit. These dedicated heroes should be treasured for not selling out, instead deciding to work independently from the stronghold of the perpetrators that try to ostracise and persecute them for always throwing a spanner in their plans of manufacturing a nation manipulated into total conformity, a nation that doesn't question authority, one dependant on direction and totally absent of critical thinking.

Another notorious technique used by the mainstream media is labelling. It is a weapon at their disposal to make or break a person, group or organisation. To portray them in whatever views that fit their agenda. There are many examples in history where this type of misrepresentation was used to rally support against someone deemed a terrorist for example, Nelson Mandela who at the time was no more fighting for human and civil rights of his generation of people and considered a fighter for freedom. Another form of this madness is the persecution of one's seeking answers to questions that were never addressed, in some instances these are the very same journalists who are trying to do their job. See I'm not concerned about what the mainstream media is constantly talking about; I'm concerned about what they're not. Today if you do not accept the so-called official report and ask one too many questions you're considered a conspiracy theorist, you're now a wacko, a crazy person, nothing you say makes sense and everything you say should be disregarded because you should always believe what the media and government say, because they would never lie to the people. Whatever. I think the worst thing I heard just recently was the name now attributed to anyone looking for the truth which is a 'truther'. What the media has done is make it harder for anyone to break the spell of stupidity, you now look down and frown upon people that seek truth, justice and freedom as though it was a bad or forbidden thing to do. So like the dummies we are we fall for every trick and ignore, degrade, discredit, reject, ridicule, dismiss, insult, mock, stereotype and fight the very ones trying to help us to be open minded in a time of global deceit. It's so ridiculous that we're even terrified of entertaining an idea ourselves, we won't dare to mention anything for fear of being a target of ridicule as well. I don't know about you but the last time I checked, I thought telling the truth or seeking it was supposed to be a good thing.

> "The worst thing to call somebody is crazy. It's dismissive. "I don't understand this person. So they're crazy." That's bullshit. These people are not crazy. They're strong people. Maybe their environment is a little sick."
> **Dave Chappelle**

> "Freethinkers are those who are willing to use their minds without prejudice and without fearing to understand things that clash with their own customs, privileges, or beliefs. This state of mind is not common, but it is essential for right thinking…"
> **Leo Tolstoy**

> "How it is we have so much information, but know so little?"
> **Noam Chomsky**

> "The media's the most powerful entity on earth. They have the power to make the innocent guilty and to make the guilty innocent, and that's power. Because they control the minds of the masses."
> **Malcolm X**

> "Whoever controls the media, controls the mind"
> **Jim Morrison**

Fear Factor

Love, life, freedom and the pursuit of happiness are the goals of nearly everyone, I think I can quiet confidently say. But where did living in a constant state of fear ever became an option and why? Almost every day, media has us scared of every little thing that goes bump in the night and has us constantly looking over our shoulder. It's insane to believe, according to the media that you have to submit to living in fear for your life even in today's world from everyone and everything, if it's not global warming, it's terrorism, diseases, natural disasters or some lone nut-job, but in other news today is going to be a bright and sunny day. The mainstream news media is all about negativity of course with a pinch of sunshine or you might never leave your house in the morning, it's your first daily dose of scare mongering that's implanted into the psyche like a caffeine fix to help you function accordingly in society's melting pot of paranoid and delusional people.

Don't get me wrong there are real dangers in this world but there is no immediate threat to our national security from some invading force, contrary to what they would like us to believe. But that doesn't stop us being bombarded with images by the media with the threats of terrorism being planned against us which might happen at anytime and anywhere, bombarded with images, moulding their idea of what the definition of a terrorist is or what they look like, their ethnicity, how they dress, the way they speak and their beliefs. Singling out a specific religious denomination and attributing any wrongdoing by them as a terrorist act, while other wrongdoers committing the same or worse acts which are not connected to or same race of these groups are dismissed and are labelled with just having a mental condition, being a delusional, a gunman, loner, rebel or freedom fighter. This is wrong and dangerous because it becomes an automatic reaction to associate someone within a specific descriptive bracket as being a terrorist even without them having any connection to extremist organisations, having any motives or producing a shred of factual evidence of any kind. It has become a type of profiling, stereotyping, a prejudicial judgement used to dehumanise and demonise a culture of people. Terror is terror, it doesn't fit a particular look or practice, a certain religion or belief; it comes in all forms, from all cultures, countries and races, even from our own. To eradicate it we must first change our mentality and our foreign policy on it.

Fabricating reports for the purpose of inducing fear towards personal gain is itself the definition of terrorism. Terrorism is not just a group of extremist, it's also an idea used to promote fear and we have had many examples of these unlawful acts helping coerce members of the public into subjugation. Remember years ago we were told that there was a massive hole in the ozone that was getting bigger and if something wasn't done soon it would destroy us all with harmful U.V. rays? What happened to that hole, did we patch it? Everyone seemed to have forgotten but lo and behold we have another disaster looming in the last few years called global warming as the former vice president Al Gore so passionately but unconvincingly campaigned over, apparently all for nothing because it would seem this year 2013 it's been reported that the polar caps have produced about 29% more ice than the previous year according to a report from the UN Intergovernmental Panel on Climate Change (IPCC), unless they're making up those stats. I'm not saying the climate is not changing, it is and it could be reacting to man-made emissions but could it also just be a natural cycle of the Earth? That don't seem to matter much now as the former V.P. have been reported that he could become the world's first carbon billionaire after investing heavily in green energy companies, funny that. If we don't question everything we will always be taken advantage of and 9 out of 10 times its for someone's own personal gain, that's why money always seem to be the solution to avert total demise.

It all seems to be nothing more than smoke and mirrors, sleight of hand. It is a great deception of information being manipulated on the greatest stage on the planet, the TV. It's conveniently sitting in every living room beaming messages from the first thing in the morning to the last thing at night, eagerly waiting to inform us of the next monster lurking around the corner. So what's it going to be next? Let's see, it could be biological, a flu of some kind like killer cat flu, or maybe it's a natural disaster, solar flares, polar shift, an asteroid maybe, or an invasion could be on the table, but from who or where? Well the only one that can probably match the firepower of the developed world is an advanced extraterrestrial force so don't be surprised, I would not rule it out. If that's not enough so you won't be straying far from a mental breakdown as its also focused on your doorstep with gun crime, knife attacks, drug wars, gangs, rapist, burglars, car thieves, child molesters and if it's not adding insult to injury even the police is getting in on the action by beating, harassing, pepper spraying, shocking with Taser guns, intimidating and abusing their authority by arresting anyone because they can. This is another form of terrorism. The stats speak for themselves, in the Western World you are seven times more likely to be killed by police following police contact and/or being in police custody than a terrorist attack, this is highly unacceptable. I know who I'm more concerned about, no wonder people are fighting back against authority.

We refuse to believe that there can be some kind of conspiracy hatched by secret societies or organisations to take total control of everything and everyone because that's impossible, crazy talk, right? Our government and the freedom of the press would surely expose any schemes being plotted against humanity, wouldn't they? Well if what they are doing is in our interest and what they are telling us is the truth, then why is everything in such a mess? Why persecute whistleblowers? Why suppress information? Why all the secrecy? People don't want to believe that there are secret forces working against them in their own institutions because it's unnatural, immoral, unjust, and unconstitutional and as one president J.F.K. said, "secrecy is repugnant in a free and open society". The mind has problems trying to process these conflicting information from what the mainstream media say and what is being done to us periodically while we continue to accept everything as though its fine, this is what's referred to as Cognitive Dissonance where your belief in the system and belief in morality, facts and logic goes to battle and the latter surrenders.

> "If you're not careful, the newspapers will have you hating the people who are being oppressed, and loving the people who are doing the oppressing."
>
> **Malcolm X**

> "I learned that courage was not the absence of fear, but the triumph over it. The brave man is not he who does not feel afraid, but he who conquers that fear."
>
> **Nelson Mandela**

> "I believe that every single event in life happens in an opportunity to choose love over fear."
>
> **Oprah Winfrey**

"He who has overcome his fears will truly be free."

Aristotle

"Fear is the path to the dark side, fear leads to anger, anger leads to hate, hate leads to suffering."

Yoda

Chapter 9

Religious Beliefs

Ancient Religion

In the beginning it is written God created man amongst many other things and well, man created religion. Well at least we can definitely say that about the more recent ones we've been practicing for the last couple thousand years, but what do we really know about the religions of the ancients? Our ancient past like that of the Egyptians and the Sumerians that date back anywhere from about 6,000 to 10,000 years and who knows for sure some archaeologist say it could be much older. We are still beginning to understand their culture and beliefs. Today the general public know very little about what was documented literally in stone and practiced not just as a religion but a way of life. Our arrogance to even suggest that their religious beliefs are nothing more than a myth and our religion is real only comes from our lack of understanding to interpret the symbolism, astrology, science and the origins of their beginning, after all they depicted a complete and accurate diagram of our solar system thousands of years before we even knew these planets existed or that the earth was round and it orbited the sun. How could they know this? To start to even try understanding the origins of the ancients we need to look at what was left as evidence, so we need to go back to the first people that invented the written word; discovered somewhere around the mid-eighteen century, written on thousands of clay tablets in a form of writing called Cuneiform. Most people have never heard of the Sumerians which is probably due to their controversial recorded history, though there are vast amounts of evidence left by the culture. Thousands of clay tablets amongst other artefacts were found in Sumer which is the land between the Euphrates and Tigris rivers, with Mesopotamia to the north and the Persian Gulf to the south, in what is known in this present-day Iraq, some claim this is the location of where the Biblical Garden of Eden was situated.

When you begin to examine what the Sumerians wrote about, you can compare the similarities to that which is written in the Bible about God with the only difference being, one is describing a God as a spiritual, all knowing, all powerful, infallible being and the other of an advance people somewhat like us but from another world, yep aliens. They wrote of an extraterrestrial people that came here to this planet many thousands of years ago from another world which had a cycle that travelled across our solar system, a planet with a cycle of 3,600 years. When this planet they called Nibiru came back within our solar cycle the ancient astronauts as they are called by some, came to our planet to explore for minerals because their atmosphere was failing and somehow this could help restore it. While on earth they came across prehistoric man which they thought could be used as miners but they were too primitive in their development so they performed genetic manipulation using their own DNA to create man in their image and likeness. Before you say this is impossible and begin to dismiss it as nothing more than myth, take a look at what we're capable of today in the field of biology and genetics, we can now grow human tissue, manipulate genomes and even clone life. This written evidence can be corroborated by some expert archaeologist with years of experience on the Sumerians, their culture, language and beliefs like Zecharia Sitchin who translated large volumes of their ancient cuneiform text and wrote many books on the subject of their origins.

As their story goes, these visitors passed on their knowledge of astrology, mathematics, language and agriculture amongst other things. The Sumerians referred to these visitors as the Anunnaki, when translated apparently means those who from the heavens came. Offspring was also produced by the Anunnaki from having relations with humans which funny enough is also in the Bible which leads me to believe that these early recordings of their creation story and others like the Mahabharata of ancient India, the Enuma Elish of ancient Babylon, the Epic of Gilgamesh from ancient Mesopotamia and others which have all been passed down from century to century and culture to culture were later being interpreted in different ways also like that of the similarities between ancient Greeks and the Roman creation stories, maybe losing its original message along the way. But what about the omitted scriptures of the Bible like the scriptures according to Enoch? Wasn't it written that Enoch walked with God? Surely Enoch must have some very interesting things to say. I would suggest anyone to look up these scriptures of Enoch as it was not included into the Bible, (I wonder why?) It speaks of a man flying around the Earth probably in a spacecraft, looking down on the planet and making a record of his experiences. Don't get me wrong I'm not saying it is true, I don't know if an advanced extraterrestrial race of beings came to earth and created mankind who have been mistaken as Gods and worshiped for centuries, although I have heard of stranger stories before and it does make us have to ask a few questions. After all where did God come from? Not Earth right, so theoretically "God" whoever he, she or they may be is by definition an extraterrestrial, which simply means one that is not of this planet.

Like the Sumerians the Ancient Egyptians also believed in and practiced a polytheistic religion, with anthropomorphic deities representing cosmic and terrestrial forces in their world but the Egyptians viewed death very differently. They believed in life after death, that they would be resurrected and judged and if their heart weighed that of a feather they would live forever amongst the Gods, yet another belief that is also reflected in the Bible. To this day we are still trying to figure out the advanced knowledge the Egyptians must have had to construct one of the world's most complex and amazing engineering feats of mathematical precision, it makes you wonder how could the ancients even be viewed as primitive at all? Archaeologist have committed their entire life to the study of the Ancient Egyptians, so much so they created an academic discipline for this type of research called Egyptology. Archaeologist studies of this type have not been conducted with any other culture or people in the world to this day. Why Egypt, why is there so much mystery surrounding these ancient people, why so many unanswered questions about where exactly did they acquire their vast knowledge or how did the Ancient Egyptians and why did they really build the pyramids? As there are no records, no blueprints, no logical explanation of how it was built and there was no Pharaoh's sarcophagus found within, no personal possessions, nor any coffin texts was even present in the pyramids. These things along with the deceased Pharaohs were only ever found in the Valley Of The Kings.

The Egyptian religion shows many distinct parallels to our modern day beliefs mentioned in the Bible. The Pharaoh Akhenaten noted for abandoning traditional Egyptian polytheism and introducing worship which was monotheistic, one supreme God, the Aten giving the solar deity a status above mere Gods. Akhenaten you can say was the forefather of monotheistic religion, but this ultimately caused a divide in Egypt. Maybe this could explain the great Exodus as a city was then built in upper Egypt as the new capital of the Pharaoh solely dedicated to his new religion and worship to the Aten but later when Akhenaten died the old religion was then revived. Akhenaten's monotheistic religion with Ra being merged with the first, original God Horus, was believed to rule in all parts of the created world, the sky, the earth, and the underworld now as Amun-Ra. In modern day Christian worship we still glorify the name of Amun or Amen after our prayer just like the Ancient Egyptians did. This brings us to the other similarities between one of the oldest and most significance of the Ancient Egyptian Gods Horus before the amalgamation with Ra and the Christian God Jesus which are very compelling, it's as though it was copied with just the names and places being changed, with some being:

1) The Trinity, father, son and Holy Ghost Vs Osiris, Isis and Horus;
2) The Immaculate Conception Vs the virgin birth;
3) The Ankh Vs The Cross;
4) Both having twelve disciples;
5) Both Baptised at age 30;
6) Was both crucified and resurrected 3 days later;
7) Was both known as The Lamb of God, as the Good Shepherd and the Word;
8) Both born on the 25th December;
9) They're both depicted as a baby in the arms of their sacred virgin mother;
10) Both performed miracles.

These similarities of the Ancient Egyptian religion and Christianity are not the only recorded comparisons but most religious beliefs that followed after Egypt did as well. They reflect elements from the tales of other deities recorded in this widespread area, such as many of the following world saviours and sons of God, all of whom also predate the Christian beliefs like that of Krishna, Mithra, Prometheus, Tammuz, Zoroaster etc. These deities, all with a birthday of 25th December signifies astrological events where the position of the sun is at its lowest point in the sky ushering in the winter equinox. The sun remains at the same position or "dead" in the sky until the third day where it appears risen to a higher point in the sky or heavens. This was known to the ancients as the rebirth of the sun which at the time was worshiped as a solar deity, so believe what you will but if you take the time to do some research and look at the factual evidence, written in stone right in front your eyes you will see that without a doubt, all religion is based on nothing more than celestial bodies and astronomical events. They all follow The Great Year, also known as the Earth's precession of the equinox in relation to the position of the Sun or the Son of God in relation to the Twelve Houses of the Zodiac or Twelve Disciples which goes through one such complete processional cycle in a period of approximately between 21,500 and 26,000 years which would bring us into a new aeon or age. This new age today is taking us out of the zodiac sign Pisces, symbolised by a fish which is attributed to Jesus in Christianity and into the zodiac sign Aquarius, symbolised by the man pouring water from an urn or as the water barer. If this is correct we might soon see a new deity, who will personify this new cosmic sign is yet to be seen. "We don't see things as they are, we see them as we are." It is a quote from Anais Nin which purports the idea that truth, the truth that one perceives, is subjective and can be wrong. What if there is no absolute truth? What if there are just degrees and misinterpretations of truth or they are lies that we just tell ourselves until we're convinced enough to believe it? Your beliefs are the greatest enemy of truth. Like religion and history.

"Facts do not cease to exist because they are ignored."
Aldous Huxley – Proper Studies

"Religion is the impotence of the human mind to deal with occurrences it cannot understand."
Karl Marx

"The more I learn about the universe, the less convinced I am that there's any sort of benevolent force that has anything to do with it, at all."

Neil deGrasse Tyson

"All that we have invented, the symbols in the church, the rituals, they are all put there by thought. Thought has invented these things. Invented the saviour. Invented the temples of India and the contents of the temples. Thought has invented all these things called sacred. You cannot deny that. So thought in itself is not sacred. And when thought invents God, God is not sacred. So what is sacred? That can only be understood or happen when there is complete freedom, from fear, from sorrow, and when there is this sense of love and compassion with its own intelligence. Then when the mind is utterly still, that which is sacred can take place."

Jiddu Krishnamurti

Gods

I always get confused when people ask me, do you believe in God? I have no idea which God they're talking about. There are so many Gods worshiped by so many religions it's hard to keep track of how many there really are, and everyone believes the one they worship, that their God, is the one true God. The very word God itself is ridiculous to me, it is such a vague and open definition, it lacks any real substance for describing what is supposed to be a supreme spiritual being, who is omnipotent and omniscient, a totally infallible creator, this is what we would like to think the word God represents. If that were true, how did he (if God is male) make so many mistakes and why would he demand our worship anyway if one was all powerful? He almost sounds indecisive and insecure to me and being who God is said to be, surely he would have seen all this mess coming when he first decided to create man, this you could say was his mistake number 1. Then there is the issue of immortality, mistake number 2. See if man obeyed everything God said and did not eat the forbidden fruit we would have all lived forever, being fruitful and multiplying, right? But where would all the trillions of people live on Earth if no one ever died? Seems like the initial plan was destined to fail from the start so instead maybe, just maybe God intentionally placed that tree in the middle of the garden in such an easily accessible place with fruit that looked so good and tasty just to deliberately kill us off. Then why did he get so upset and kicked us out of paradise for eating it or was he just pretending and this was all part of his grand master plan as well? What about mistake number

3? The Serpent, the Devil himself; why did God let him live after being betrayed by him; or why even create him in the first place? These are just a few things that have me scratching my head about what is written in the Bible and taken as gospel by many religions, which leads me to question the accuracy of the translation and the content. Maybe that's why there are so many different religious beliefs based on so many different versions coming out of one book, everyone's far too confused.

In the beginning God created the Heavens and the Earth, this is the very first line from the Bible and the translation is apparently wrong. How could the first line, the first words translated be incorrect? Therefore this sets precedence for misleading the reader, especially someone who believes these words to be the words inspired by the almighty himself. The mistranslated word in this line I refer to is "God", which was translated from the original Hebrew Scriptures. The Hebrew word in the original text is "Elohim", now it doesn't take a language scholar to look up the correct translation of this word especially taking into consideration the importance of this one word in the Bible. Elohim means Gods and El or Eli means God, notice one is plural, meaning many and the other signifies the singular, meaning one. So I guess my question is, why the deliberate mistranslation changing Gods to God? It was as though someone was trying to conceal what the author intended and was trying to establish their own version of events, opinion and belief of a monotheistic, one supreme God, like that of the Egyptian Pharaoh Akhenaten. There are other examples of "Gods" in the scriptures where there are gatherings of the Gods and meetings conducted, though some may say that those were in fact Angels, huh? Then why say Gods, and what exactly are Angels anyway?

Well apparently Angels are not Gods but they are Godlike, they are deemed as supernatural beings or spirits, usually depicted as benevolent celestial beings with wings, who act as intermediaries between Heaven and Earth, or as guardian spirits or a guiding influence by carrying out God's tasks, so basically God's servants, but I thought that's what we were? How would you know an Angel from God or the Devil for that matter if one appeared before you? I guess you couldn't really know unless they actually told you who they were, but we all have preconceived ideas of what they look like, no thanks to ancient depictions, myths, mistranslations, popular culture, movies and TV. A winged spiritual being doesn't seem to be the actual meaning that was intended for the word Angel when I did a bit of research into the origin of the word, the languages it was translated from, depictions and the mythology of the ancients. The original word came from the Hebrew Scriptures which is Mal'ach, this simply means "Messenger" in English. When it was first translated into Greek their word for messenger was "Angelos". It was then simply converted using the English language version "Angel" that we still continue to use today with of course the attached supernatural attributes of wings which are sometimes depicted in the movies instead of using the true meaning, just a person with a message, a messenger. This was also done to the man, the prophet, the teacher, once called Yehoshua.

And who is Yehoshua you ask? Well he was just a man with a message as well, a teacher, a healer, a philosopher, a prophet, one that understood the great mystery and importance of life itself, who was willing to share with those that would listen. But this idea was hijacked whether intentionally or not by the Romans of all people and rebranded as Jesus by the Roman Catholic Church, a deity which some Christians still debate to this day if he was indeed God or just the son of God. Another issue I've got amongst other things is with the name Jesus Christ, firstly Christ is not a name, it's a title which was given to many a deity throughout the centuries i.e. Sol Invictus "Unconquered Sun" who was the official Sun God of the later Roman Empire and the date of 25th December which we celebrate as Christmas was selected in order to correspond with the Roman festival of Dies Natalis Solis Invicti, or "Birthday of the Unconquered Sun", a coincidence? Of course not. Then there is the Latin name Jesus which they gave to the prophet, why the name change from Yehoshua? In the English accepted version of the name Jesus derives from the Latin name Iesus, which transliterates the Greek name Iēsoûs, so it is easy to see where we adopted the name by replacing the I with a J, but it is not a direct English translation, cause if it were, the name of Yehoshua when directly translated into English from Hebrew would mean "I am saviour".

It's not that I don't believe in a creator, I do. And it's not that I believe only in evolution, I don't. There is some truth in evolution and I have no doubt that we were created; however I believe that for myself or anyone else to claim to know without a doubt who or what the creator is would be highly unethical as there is no evidence to prove this claim over another. The problem I'm having is the religious dogma accepted by many without question or the need for reason and facts. The very definition of a God is anything or anyone you believe to be a supreme being, worthy of your worship and this being acceptable to me is ludicrous and I'll tell you why. Some people worship objects you might say that's Idolatry, some the heavenly bodies like the sun which is known as Paganism, some the Earth known as mother Gaia, some the Virgin Mary others Jesus but all these personal Gods have one thing in common, they were or still are actually someone or something psychical, something real, something they can see, feel, understand and relate to and though I may not agree, I fully understand. This connection gives one hope. Finally the idea of one supreme God, all seeing, all knowing, the Alfa and Omega, infallible, all loving, all caring, master of the universe with a divine plan, who will someday bring peace and everlasting life in a paradise without death, fear, pain and hate, once you're good and obey his laws you go to heaven or you'll burn forever and ever in hell (although I would like to see how a soul can burn) is a romantic fallacy. For one to imply that everything which happens is all part of God's eternal plan is an insult and defamation of God's character, when considering the grave atrocities committed on this Earth. I just wonder, couldn't whoever God is just simply have done it right from the very beginning and save us all these aeon's of agony and grief?

> "I prayed for freedom for twenty years, but received no answer until I prayed with my legs."
> **Frederick Douglass - Autobiographies**

> "I cannot imagine a God who rewards and punishes the objects of his creation, whose purposes are modelled after our own,- a God, in short, who is but a reflection of human frailty. Neither can I believe that the individual survives the death of his body, although feeble souls harbour such thoughts through fear or ridiculous egotisms."
> **Albert Einstein**

> "I believe in God, but not as one thing, not as an old man in the sky. I believe that what people call God is something in all of us. I believe that what Jesus and Mohammed and Buddha and all the rest said was right. It's just that the translations have gone wrong."
> **John Lennon**

> "You bear God within you, poor wretch, and know it not."
> **Epictetus**

> "Everything in the universe is within you. Ask all from yourself"
> **-Rumi**

Our Hidden Past

If history has thought us anything is that it can sometimes be absolutely wrong. We learn of the world's ancient past and events from men and women committed to finding the truth of our origins and man's journey to the present by the observations and evidence found which are then examined, documented, preserved and sometimes showcased for our benefit. Though some are interested in uncovering only truth others can be coerced by their prejudice views, fear of being discredited, influenced by global recognition or just out to plainly suppress information that doesn't correlate with their theories and beliefs also of what consequences may arise due to certain other influential parties interest, like that of Charles Dawson whose falsified specimens which was later discredited as fakes once a proper analysis had been undertaken. It is no secret that archaeological and geological evidence have been overlooked, ignored, forged, destroyed, fabricated, misinterpreted, mistranslated or hidden away from the public before and is still being done to this day for own selfish reasons and personal gain. As archaeologist make new discoveries and new technologies for examining evidence are developed our history books have had to be revised as some findings were proven to being falsified and/or inaccurate therefore leaving some text to no longer be seen as a viable source for accurate information after the new evidence uncovered now contradicts the old findings, even though some are still being used as learning materials to this day. I'm not saying all theories of our history is totally wrong but we now know what we do from the scientific facts gained from the specimens we possess. What I am saying is inevitably as we make new discoveries and they are made public, opinions about our theories of human history will definitely have to change.

I say theory because that's all it is, a theory for now as nothing can be proven as absolute when it comes to the great debate about how our human evolution/creation story began, about the formation of the Earth and life in general. These are only opinions agreed upon by a majority that came to similar conclusions from all the evidence which have been found and examined to this date, but what about the ones that suggest otherwise, artefacts that are seldom mentioned, or fossils that haven't been unearthed as yet and what secrets do they hold which can give us a different perspective on our origins? The one important thing that have yet to be found and frustrating archaeologist from proving without a doubt that we actually evolved from a single cell organism all the way to the human beings we are today as a fact, is one specimen from the group what's known as transitional fossils with the most important of the collection still undiscovered called the missing link. There's probably a good reason why we have found thousands of dinosaur bones, fossils of other extinct creatures and even the ancient Neanderthals dating back hundreds of thousands of years but still struggle to find the all illusive transitional fossil that directly links the last and most conclusive stage of evolution completing the transition to modern day man. You would think there will be hundreds if not thousands of completely intact remains scattered everywhere on earth just waiting to be dug up especially as they are not as old as all the other ancient specimens found to date, but no, not one has ever been identified, why? Maybe it doesn't exist, but if that's true what does that mean about how we developed or came to be the way we are today?

There are many ancient evidence scattered about all over this planet that are seldom talked about for the simple reason, it just can't be explained, no one knows what it is, how or why it was done. What's annoying me is the people that try to present this evidence which is available, in a logical manner, bringing alternative ideas, allowing you to think outside the box of conventional theories that seem impossible to explain, are instead ridiculed and not even mentioned in the mainstream media like that of Erich von Däniken the author of numerous books which has sold about 65 million worldwide. He has also been awarded many distinctions for his extensive research, books and work carried out over the years. He describes his interpretation of Gods and the origin of mankind in his first book published in 1968, Chariots Of The Gods. I wonder if you have ever heard of him before? I was like most people and I just assumed what we're told was probably true, it was only after I began to examine these accepted theories for myself things didn't add up. There is the obvious unanswered questions that remains a mystery but even the ones to which expert explanation is given of how or why certain structures were possibly constructed they begin to sound absolutely preposterous. To this day you can ask any so-called professional in their field of expertise about how these phenomenal achievements in ancient construction, scattered all across the globe can even be possible and they'll admit to you, that they just don't know.

When we look at ancient cultures we tend to think of them as unsophisticated, uncivilised, uneducated, savages, it's what we were made to believe from reading our history books. Civilisation in our eyes, in our culture when looking in from the outside, of others living in conditions different form our own may appear chaotic and primitive but they managed to live in harmony with their environment unlike us. We see them as primitive only because we fail to understand their cultures and beliefs or maybe it is an attempt to suppress their history and what they actually knew. Modern civilisation is no more civilised than our ancestors were. It would seem it's probably less so. It doesn't take a genius to work out our entire global economy is monopolised, creating misery, war, famine, poverty, crime and slaves to debt. It is the main cause of all social ills but yet we pretend that we are somehow better today because we have money, technology, we can come home to a microwave dinner and TV shows. Well if that's the case then how does everything seem to be spiralling towards total oblivion? When we do our research about our ancient history we will come to a realisation that the Sumerians, Ancient Egyptians, Mayans, Aztecs, Ancient Indians and Chinese cultures etc. acquired knowledge way beyond our understanding. This is undeniable. Their texts, inscriptions, architecture, paintings, monuments, traditions, beliefs etc. are the only evidence left from which we are still trying to learn the truth about their way of life. This has brought me to the conclusion that it can only be one of two things, one is that we are still to dumb to figure out what the ancients knew thousands of years ago, or two, some have acquired this knowledge and it's their intention to keep what they've learnt from us so they may keep us in total ignorance and confusion, probably in order to control us and attain absolute power over the world and humanity. One of these two options has to be right otherwise we would've learnt from our past mistakes in history and would prevent ourselves from making these same mistakes over and over, constantly and horrifically from ever being repeated.

> "All knowledge that is about human society, and not about the natural world, is historical knowledge, and therefore rests upon judgment and interpretation. This is not to say that facts or data are nonexistent, but that facts get their importance from what is made of them in interpretation… for interpretations depend very much on who the interpreter is, who he or she is addressing, what his or her purpose is, at what historical moment the interpretation takes place."
> **Edward W. Said**

"The most effective way to destroy people is to deny and obliterate their own understanding of their history."

"He who controls the past controls the future. He who controls the present controls the past."
George Orwell-1984

"History is always written by the winners. When two cultures clash, the loser is obliterated, and the winner writes the history books-books which glorify their own cause and disparage the conquered foe."
Dan Brown

"The highest form of ignorance is when you reject something you don't know anything about"
Wayne W. Dyer

"Half of writing history is hiding the truth."
Joss Whedon

CHAPTER 10

Free Your Mind

Community & Trust

When the great economic crash comes, and trust me it will eventually unless a new system replaces this current one, once you have come to understand the inner workings of the nation's money creation by the central and private banks it seems now to be only a matter of when and not if and the only use we'll have left for our paper money is wiping our butts. The people will have no choice but to resort into a pure chaotic state and an everyman for themselves kind of scenario will ensue. Everyone will look to protect the little valuables and commodities they have left while trying to acquire a bit more for survival, mainly food. It's only natural, but how exactly will this be possible without money to purchase anything? There is the very risky option of looting and stealing but that's not right or moral in fact it's downright stupid and dangerous. Hoarded wealth will now become worthless and no one will trade their essential food for gold or any other form of so-called precious metals or stones as they are notoriously impossible for the digestive system to break down as you may know. It need not come to this, having to resort to acting out of pure desperation. Instead we can start by creating a community, one that's prepared to work together, one built on responsibility and trust.

As we look around our neighbourhood we notice how closely we live amongst each other but seldom interact or act in unison, why is that? I'm not talking about the odd neighbour next door that we sometimes borrow a drill from or jump start our car when needed, I'm referring to everyone around us, everyone we interact with, everyone like minded and everyone we know. These people are in the same situation just like you. They are also struggling to maintain a living and seeing it getting worse as time goes on. Maybe our stressful lifestyles has us far too busy, preventing us from engaging in matters that can directly affect us and our families welfare or maybe we've become weary of other people, afraid to interact, fear for our security, lack of trust, is it our differences in race, religion, political views, class, culture or is it all of the above? These are the reasons why society is so divided in opinions and why it makes the decisions it does, trying to preserve what sanctity it thinks it has left. We must put aside our trivial beliefs and work together on what's most important which is being able to live free, in peace and with a chance to prosper.

Let's face it; nothing we have done in the last century has worked to bring a sustainable economy and the betterment of all the people. This system has manufactured a segregation of the classes with commercial and political capitalism forcing people to be economically oppressed thus creating an underclass of society. We all play along abiding by the rules of the game, throw our dice and hope we come up trumps, aren't you tired of always losing? I would like to win for a change but it's impossible to win when the game is fixed, cause in a monopoly like what this is, the banker always wins. I'm afraid it's up to you now however you see fit to deal with the unfortunate events that are rapidly approaching. The good thing is there are always many options available which you can resort to. Some of your options may suffice for a time, or you can chose to do nothing by putting your faith in the system and hope for the best, that the government will sort it out which I seriously doubt as I'm sure they'll have some suggestions in mind which they are probably itching to implement. How about giving absolute power to the ruling class while coping with ever diminishing liberties, justice and freedom while enslaved with a country's unmanageable debt, no? Somehow I didn't think so.

I believe the best option of escaping the inevitable economic crisis is to create our own viable and sustainable economic and even a financial segment of society to operate alongside this parasite of a system. It won't be by no part an easy one to achieve. We must first have an organised and committed people willing to place their trust in each other and requiring the voluntary involvement of an entire community toward the creation of their very own new monetary system. Once established with the agreement of its members it can be one without restriction, able to grow and expand nationally maybe even internationally, one designed to operate freely without the reliance upon just government bank notes only. It will be traded as an alternative source of currency in conjunction with the existing central bank notes which is a concept already in use in some towns of the United Kingdom like Sussex, Devon and Brixton. This idea has been implemented since 2009 with over 80 local businesses accepting the currency, so it's not some new, crazy idea as you may have first thought. By creating a new currency we will always have the ability to exchange it for services within our community provided by tradesmen like plumbers, bricklayers, mechanics, carpenters etc. We will also have the opportunity to acquire the necessities especially like food and medicine but most importantly these notes will belong to the people, free of accruing any interest therefore free of any debt whatsoever, giving them a voice that will be impossible to ignore, in turn empowering them to bring about real change, on their journey to real freedom.

"The secret of change is to focus all of your energy, not on fighting the old, but on building the new."

Socrates

"Power concedes nothing without a demand. It never did and it never will. Find out just what any people will quietly submit to and you have found out the exact measure of injustice and wrong which will be imposed upon them, and these will continue till they are resisted with either words or blows, or with both. The limits of tyrants are prescribed by the endurance of those whom they oppress."

Frederick Douglass - 1857

"In the end, we will remember not the words of our enemies, but the silence of our friends."

"An individual has not started living until he can rise above the narrow confines of his individualistic concerns to the broader concerns of all humanity."

Martin Luther King Jr

Freedom

How free are you? Do you feel free? I mean do you feel free enough to do with your life as you please, without any restrictions, without the need for anyone's permission, to forge your own destiny? You might say yes you do, we'll as long as we abide by the laws laid down by society we can do whatever we want, we'll maybe not everything, but at least we have a democracy, right? Unlike China or Saudi Arabia you can say we have more freedom than some, so shouldn't we count ourselves lucky? More freedom than some you say? This is where the conversation gets you to the realisation that you are not indeed totally free as you may think and maybe, just maybe there are more restrictions and control upon your existence and livelihood than you even realised.

You have to ask ourselves if we're so free, can we chose wherever we would like to live and just go there, not have to give up part of our earnings as taxes, can we practice our trade without restrictions, without permits, travel without identification documents in our car, a plane or ship or why do we need ID at all, can we say in public what we really think or feel although it can offend, can we protect ourselves and our families lives from intruders with the use of deadly force if need be, source food naturally in forests, rivers or lakes unhampered, can we go anywhere to marry anyone we love of any gender if desired, can we experiment with mind altering drugs on ourselves without persecution and prosecution, are we allowed to take our own life if terminally ill and suffering or for any other reason in fact, can we use our own choice of natural medicines in the benefit of our health, must we comply with all the statutes, acts and codes created by man although we may disagree with most of them or find them excessive and unfair? The point I'm trying to make is, whether you agree or disagree to all these questions as being your God given rights to exercise or not, you still have no say in the outcome. Now you realise you're definitely not as free as you first thought.

There is without a doubt the universal law, Natural Law which is, don't cause harm or loss to anyone or their property and if by accident you did, you must act responsibly and be accountable for all your actions, right the wrong so to speak, anything else which you decide to do with your life should be entirely up to you and not the will of the state. Everything outside of natural law is manmade, fictitious constructs representing an alternative reality, the beginning of implementing a totalitarian state. It's the esoteric messages portrayed in films like Alice In Wonderland, The Matrix and The Wonderful Wizard of Oz. If you haven't read the original works or seen the movie I suggest you do. It is to control a nation of people towards A New World Order, an implementing of a 1984, Orwellian like state, being coerced into a situation, idea, or societal condition that George Orwell identified as being destructive to the welfare of a free and open society. It connotes an attitude and a policy of control by propaganda, surveillance, misinformation, denial of truth, and manipulation of the past which has become undeniably apparent today. This is why I adhere to the common law not law by man, statutes forced upon me are unlawful to my absolute freedom, why? Take slavery for example, it is an ugly stain on history that is preferred to be forgotten by some, remember this immoral and repugnant act was once accepted by law. All law by man does not mean that all law is absolute if it is not just to all man.

When we look around the world we live in today, it is apparent to see that we are being treated more like property and not people. Though we may protest about government decisions which go against our every will, it continually falls on the deaf ears of politicians, then to protect themselves and their selfish interest they initiate a response of the riot police, their instruments to establish order. These police fail to realise that they too are a part of this betrayed family but they still carry out their orders precisely and effectively like that of the German Stormtroopers to literally bash and break your efforts, your spirit and a few skulls in the process, moulding you back into conformity. Monitoring and collecting information is another form of managing ones property, surveillance cameras, passports and identification cards are means of tracking your movements and of what exactly you might be up to. If that wasn't going far enough there's also the National Security Agency (N.S.A.) and the Government Communications Headquarters (G.C.HQ.) that tap into all your personal electronic devices, listening to your conversations, reading emails and text messages, spying on networking websites and even pinpointing your locations at any time using G.P.S. The Government's unjustified, immoral and blatant disregard for our privacy and liberty tells me that there is no such thing as total freedom in this contrived version of society which has all of the attributes of modern day slavery.

When you mention slavery people tend to think of it in the conventional sense, of being in bondage, violated, raped, used and abused, whipped, lynched and deprived of every god given human right there is but there are other forms of slavery, some going on this very moment, one that controls you and compels you to be something you are not, sometimes to be someone that you don't even want to be but it is done to you just the same, very cleverly, without you even being aware that you are indeed a slave to the world's order. Our contribution to the system comes naturally because of this conditioning by society, though sometimes we dislike or are unhappy with the roles attributed to us cause it's not what we intended for ourselves and as a result we can't help but hate our jobs, it becomes tedious, demoralizing and destructive to the mind, body and soul. Other choices available systematically diminish, left with no other options we're forced to labour on just so we may afford to live. The sole purpose of society's design is for your participation within the workforce, to earn just enough money in order to survive. We participate with society's predetermined order because basically it's all we've been offered and come to know and these options are becoming even more limited or undesirable. So unless you were entertaining the idea of relocating to some remote part of unclaimed land in the wilderness, where it would enable us to exempt ourselves from converting to participate within the system of things, we're trapped in it. Absconding from society into complete solitude would be ok for some, but that doesn't solve the problems we face now nor does it benefit our family, friends or the future liberty, freedom and prosperity of mankind.

The goal that we must strive toward is a free, fair and open society for all, not one that manufactures a working class for the sake of producing commodities or solely revenue creation and for profit, not one based upon a class divided by the accumulation of wealth, not one that deprives its people of human and civil rights. Together we must make a stand to fight for the betterment of all not just some. First there must be a revolution of the self, an awakening in consciousness to recognize that it is us that must change initially if we are to ever bring about the change we wish to see, a paradigm shift. Create a movement, a movement for change in social and economic injustice that's an advocate for peace, unity, and all that's just. It can be achievable once the people realise that the true power of a nation resides with them and not a government, not an institution, nor a corporation but it must be organised around a common idea towards a common goal. Great tidal-waves of change have come before and will come again. We only have to look at the past for inspiration from great men and women that made a stand in times of tribulation, which personally are sometimes costly but nonetheless they have paved a way and drawn a blueprint which we can use as an example to follow, like that of Martin Luther King Jr, Malcolm X, Mahatma Gandhi, Nelson Mandela, Rosa Parks, Susan B. Anthony, Frederick Douglass, Harriet Tubman, Ernesto Guevara and Hugo Chávez to name a few who will be forever seen as revolutionist that changed the world, which was once thought to be unchangeable.

> "I am free, no matter what rules surround me. If I find them tolerable, I tolerate them; if I find them too obnoxious, I break them. I am free because I know that I alone am morally responsible for everything I do."
> **Robert A. Heinlein**

> "Marxism taught me what society was. I was like a blindfolded man in a forest, who doesn't even know where north or south is. If you don't eventually come to truly understand the history of the class struggle, or at least have a clear idea that society is divided between the rich and the poor, and that some people subjugate and exploit other people, you're lost in a forest, not knowing anything."
> **Fidel Castro**

> "The most important kind of freedom is to be what you really are. You trade in your reality for a role. You trade in your sense for an act. You give up your ability to feel, and in exchange, put on a mask. There can't be any large-scale revolution until there's a personal revolution, on an individual level. It's got to happen inside first."
> **Jim Morrison**

"Disobedience is the true foundation of liberty. The obedient must be slaves."

Henry David Thoreau

"I am not a liberator. Liberators do not exist. The people liberate themselves."

Ernesto Guevara

"Emancipate yourselves from mental slavery. None but ourselves can free our minds."

Bob Marley

"Liberties aren't given, they are taken."

Aldous Huxley

"It is hard to free fools from the chains they revere."

Voltaire

"Free your mind."

Morpheus

Reality Check

"And you shall know the truth, and the truth shall make you free."

A quote that couldn't be more true and relevant to these times, it is the quintessential requirement that could end all animosity and regression embroiled in humankind's existence. The apocalypse is at hand, not in the biblical sense but by what it actually means, a disclosure of knowledge, a lifting of the veil or a revelation where what is hidden will come to light. Today we have the internet, one of the best methods for gaining a vast amount of information that would otherwise be restricted, ignored, covered up and suppressed. It has spawned a new kind of pro-info warrior, one whom is dedicated to getting the people informed about activities that would otherwise be preferred kept secret by private entities and our governments, as to what exactly they're doing to you and in your name. We know so much already, we know what our governments are doing, what the major corporations and oligarchs do, what banking institutions, power, media, money and unconstitutional laws are doing to us and this planet, isn't this not enough to get angry about, so why are we not all acting now to stop this madness and prevent this from ever happening to anyone, anywhere again? It would seem these days that exposing illegal and corrupt activities against the powers that be could get you labelled a traitor and thrown into prison for a very long time or worse, it's no wonder most people are deeply afraid of going against the system. It's by using that fear of what we believe may happen to us that they try to keep everyone in check with.

To rule or to govern by fear, intimidation and treats of persecution is the method which was used by slave owners over their property to attain total submissiveness that they may not rebel against their masters or even contemplate trying to escape, some even came to revere their enslavement and dread their emancipation. So does your government use a structure designed around gaining conformity from fear of punishment? Of course they do. When you're afraid of being arrested, fined and penalised, imprisoned, police brutality, getting a criminal record, having property seized, losing your job or your children etc. it's easy to see the reasons why we have such a compliant society unwilling to step outside of what they're told, but for some enough is enough. If any government or institution requires compliance by force through fear and intimidation then they obviously have no authority nor they deserve any or they would not use such coercive and draconian means to establish their rule, it's about high time we break this cycle. One option available to us is whistle-blowing, it's an act that has come out of sheer frustration due to the unlawful acts and the abuses of authority being ever continuous, where justice always seem to turn a blind eye and towards those that seem untouchable by law. When we stand idly by and chose to do nothing when confronted by crime and injustice being repeatedly perpetrated against humanity, it's as though we've become part of that criminal act. Those like Private Manning, Julian Assange and Edward Snowden who refused to let themselves become implicated by these unlawful actions and instead chose to expose the corruption to the public, putting the interest of the people first even though this will come with great personal risk to themselves, they did what was right. This is yet another example to warn you about the consequences of going against authority, to stay in line, do as your told, obey.

If you were into comics when you were younger like I was, you may have come across Bizarro World, it's a fictional, cube shaped planet in the DC universe where everything is the opposite to that on earth, where there's madness and chaos, where good is bad and right is wrong. I like to believe that planet really exist but this Earth, this world we live in is Bizarro World and the other planet, well that's the normal one, it has to be, it couldn't be any other way cause what's happening in this world in my opinion is insane, there is no other word for it. Everyone can plainly see hypocrisy performed to the highest degree within the policies imposed upon society, implemented by their governments which seem to only benefit corporate interest and themselves while continually attacking the working class, low income earners and poor. Apathy amongst the people is a great concern, as well as the enmity towards our fellow man. You must understand this is exactly what those who desire power require; to have you distracted, confused, fearful and divided as much as possible. I'm positive it's what they collude about in the shadows of parliament, and dimly lit boardrooms concocting the perfect conditions needed to gain more control over society. If we do not see past our prejudicial views and opinions of others or of those less fortunate than us and continue demanding less of a benefit toward their livelihood than what we would intend for ourselves, then we'll achieve nothing and not deserve anything.

If you're still waiting for the revolution to begin then you're obviously not paying attention, the insurrection of the masses started years ago. If you haven't noticed, a global shift in consciousness is in progress, we can see the evidence of this from the coordinated and organized protests taking place in various countries around the globe against political corruption, corporate criminal activity, war, diminishing and violations of human rights, austerity, banking malpractice, capitalism, media manipulation, inequality etc. Groups of movements have sprouted in wake of this paradigm shift despite the efforts of government agencies and the mainstream media attacking and trying to suppress their voice in order to maintain their grasp onto power whilst preventing, deterring and making slanderous accusations as to oppose any support these causes may gain. The March Against Monsanto, March Against Mainstream Media, Occupy Wall Street, Anonymous, Greenpeace, Close Guantanamo, The Freeman Movement, Amnesty International etc. are a few examples of organizations dedicated to changing the world for the better which more people are snapping out of their hypnotic state and joining every day. According to the evidence left in many ancient texts, it is widely known that these early cultures calculated accurately the end of an age or an aeon, from their knowledge gained by observing the precession of the equinox they believed that entering a new cosmic age brought about change in the world and mankind, could it be a coincidence that this new age of Aquarius were now entering have anything to do with our evolutionary change in consciousness? Or maybe we're just tired of being trampled upon again and again.

Moments are all we have, it's what we live in, the right here and right now with our memories of the past, that's it. We always tend to think in terms of "time" to explain and describe the past, the present and the future, in seconds, minutes, hours, days, weeks, months and years. Time controls our life, it tells us when to wake up and when to go to bed, what day and year it is, when to eat, when to start work and even the very minute you were born, the thing is time is just another made up fiction that dictates every aspect of our life, time is not real. The year is now 2014 and if you said its four million years today you would probably be closer to the actual true age of the earth, and the age of early man is close to about two hundred thousand years, so what's today's date again? All that we experience, all which happens is only cycles, the earth is rotating and also revolving around the sun in our solar system which is in relation to the universe, not for millions but billions of years and all we've decided to record unto a calendar was only about two thousand of these cycles and somehow we managed to mess things up as badly as we did in such a tiny fraction of the worlds existence. The past is gone but it must be a lesson learnt, the moment is now to bring about the change we wish to see because the future is not set, it has yet to be written, any possible future is achievable we only need make it so. Tomorrow is only a preconceived vision, it's not yet a reality, and therefore it doesn't exist. It can only begin to materialise after we have physically laid the pathway towards that moment beginning with a conscious idea about what kind of a tomorrow we desire, not one that's expected.

With all that's said, let's not waste one more moment to quibble over and stress about things of little or no importance, let's not continue fighting to change the old system but instead build a new one, let's be more open and accepting to new ideas and to others instead of hastily dismissing and rejecting without first reasoning and making attempts in understanding. Reading and researching of the law is also pertinent to our journey that we may know what our rights are, to protect and reclaim our power over those who wish to oppress and enslave us. Let us also reclaim our true selves, our humanity, our true purpose to be the caretakers of our only home, the planet Earth and be responsible for each other's welfare and justice. To prosper as one family together tearing down all barriers racial or otherwise, not separated nor segregated from each other and still respecting the beliefs one chooses, to have complete freedom for all to enjoy not just a select few. We've all been guilty of participating in these things but do not despair, do not feel guilty, we must remember we are not perfect, we will fall; we will sometimes stray off the path. Never have any regrets about anything, no matter how bad of a mistake you've made, everyone makes mistakes. Everything that you did in the past must instead be viewed as a learning experience to understand about life and yourself. Finally to know thyself, to conquer our fears and express our feelings of pure love for each other not confusion and judgment spurned by ego and hate so we can all move forward equally together in unity and in peace.

In the end, like you, I can only be who I am and who I strive to be, I am that I am nothing more, I can only be me and my journey is mine and mine alone though the path may be one that I can't surely yet see. Reality is yours to dream, imagine, choose, create and be, but it can only begin when you take that first step through the door, leading onto the road, to a place of endless possibilities.

> "We don't want to hate and despise one another. In this world there is room for everyone, and the good earth is rich and can provide for everyone. The way of life can be free and beautiful, but we have lost the way."
> **Charles Chaplin – The Great Dictator**

> "I wanted to change the world. But I have found that the only thing one can be sure of changing is oneself."
> **Aldous Huxley – Point Counter Point**

RECREATING REALITY

My Own Favourite Quotes

I hope that by reading this you have begun to open your mind to some alternative ways of looking at our world, and that you now possess some tools with which to recreate your own reality.

Below I have carefully selected a few takeaway quotes that I feel succinctly portray the messages I aim to illustrate with this book.

> "Never have any regrets about anything, no matter how bad of a mistake you've made, everyone makes mistakes. Everything that you did in the past must instead be viewed as a learning experience to understand about life and yourself."

> "In the end, like you, I can only be who I am and who I strive to be, I am that I am nothing more, I can only be me and my journey is mine and mine alone though the path may be one that I can't surely yet see. Reality is yours to dream, imagine, choose, create and be, but it can only begin when you take that first step through the door, leading onto the road, to a place of endless possibilities."

"If we do not see past our prejudicial views and opinions of others or of those less fortunate than us and continue demanding less of a benefit toward their livelihood than what we would intend for ourselves, then we'll achieve nothing and not deserve anything."

"This is why I adhere to the common law not law by man, statutes forced upon me are unlawful to my absolute freedom, why? Take slavery for example, it is an ugly stain on history that is preferred to be forgotten by some, remember this immoral and repugnant act was once accepted by law."

"All law by man does not mean that all law is absolute if it is not just to all man"

"The mainstream news media is all about negativity of course with a pinch of sunshine or you might never leave your house in the morning, it's your first daily dose of scare mongering that's implanted into the psyche like a caffeine fix to help you function accordingly in society's melting pot of paranoid and delusional people."

"If you control the meanings, the very definitions of words, you control the collective thoughts of society."

"Tomorrow is only a preconceived vision, it's not yet a reality, and therefore it doesn't exist. It can only begin to materialise after we have physically laid the pathway towards that moment beginning with a conscious idea about what kind of a tomorrow we desire, not one that's expected."

"Majority of people form their general views, opinions, personalities, beliefs and attitudes from their environment and society. When that society then limits the spectrum of information and debate you get a population of people that lack the ability to deviate from the rhetoric of conformity due to their limited knowledge, leading to an inability of critical thinking."

"See I'm not concerned about what the mainstream media is constantly talking about; I'm concerned about what they're not."

"It's not that I don't believe in a creator, I do; or that I believe only in evolution, I don't; but there is some truth in evolution and it is without a doubt in my mind that we were created, but for me or anyone I believe to claim that they know without a doubt who or what the creator is, should be seen as highly unethical as there is no evidence to support their claim over another."

"Believe what you will but if you take the time to do some research and look at the factual evidence, written in stone right in front your eyes you will see that without a doubt, all religion is based on nothing more than celestial bodies and astronomical events."

"Terror is terror, it doesn't fit a particular look or practice, a certain religion or belief; it comes in all forms, from all cultures, countries and races, even from our own. To eradicate it we must first change our mentality and our foreign policy on it."

"Our world is nothing more than a speck in the vastness of the universe but this speck is our only home, our entire world and yet it is a great part of the universe."

"'Greed Is Good' this is the motto of international corporations. The very foundation of their empire is to carry out whatever needs to be done, by any means necessary with the sole purpose of making profits."

"I always get confused when people ask me, do you believe in God? I have no idea which God they're talking about."

"If ignorance is bliss then what is the point of knowledge?"

"If you're still wondering; what is the meaning of life? Why are we here? And what is the purpose of our existence? Then you obviously haven't experienced love yet."

"Never work for the system; instead make the system work for you."

"If you're just going to believe everything people say or always follow popular opinion, then what is the point of having instincts?"

"In order to know something I need to fully understand it, only then can I believe it to be truth, then I can have faith in it."

"Love is the only answer I could come up with when looking into, and trying to understand the pursuit of our happiness. It's surely a good enough reason. No I'm positive it's definitely

Recreating Reality

the best and only reason for everything, everything that really matters."

"You can never lie to yourself even if you try."

"People that don't understand politics vote; people that do understand politics start a revolution"

"These financial systems we're bound to are the products of the people's perceived reality brought on from our own lack of involvement and understanding about the inner working mechanisms of money creation."

"Instead of empowering us with the knowledge we need from birth to be free they designed the world in such a very clever way that it's hidden from us through misinformation and distractions that we may not only participate in our own mental enslavement but anyone or any attempt to emancipate us from our chains is seen as a threat, an enemy to the illusions of our security, justice and free will of this society."

"The only way we will ever survive this great betrayal of our true identity and break free from our hypnotic state of materialism, fear, greed and anger is to understand we are all one."

"The more self sufficient we can be; the less dependent on the monetary system we will be. This independence will empower us, great strength will bring about our total freedom, and then our future will be guaranteed."

"I guess democracy is like magic, you know that it really doesn't exist but it gives you the illusion that it is real."

"It is clear to see they're not interested in using money to eradicate poverty they're interest is eradicating people to make money."

"For one to imply that everything which happens is all part of God's eternal plan is an insult and defamation of God's character, when considering the grave atrocities committed on this Earth."

"Politics is a diabolical form of psychology and language, used against the public to confuse, trick, sway, distort, and downright lie about important information and promote their agendas making the unacceptable seem acceptable."

"We can never be truly be free if we consider someone our enemy"

"Apathy amongst the people is a great concern, as well as the enmity towards our fellow man. You must understand this is exactly what those who desire power require; to have you distracted, confused, fearful and divided as much as possible."

"The Government's unjustified, immoral and blatant disregard for our privacy and liberty tells me that there is no such thing as total freedom in this contrived version of society which has all of the attributes of modern day slavery."

"Misinformation is a great adversary to combat, but to see through the wall of deception is by far not an easy task;

the odds are highly stacked against us, it is everything, it is everywhere, and it is everyone."

"When we stand idly by and chose to do nothing when confronted by crime and injustice being repeatedly perpetrated against humanity, it's as though we've become part of that criminal act."

"Your beliefs are the greatest enemy of truth."

"The world around us is not as we believe it to be and if we were all to awaken to the corrupt system today, things would change overnight."

"Change the way you look at the world and the world changes."

R. Ryan Questel

Notes

Notes

Notes

Notes

Notes